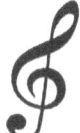

SONGWRITER'S
NOTEBOOK

...for writing lyrics and
composing music...
...for inspiration, notes,
and good ideas

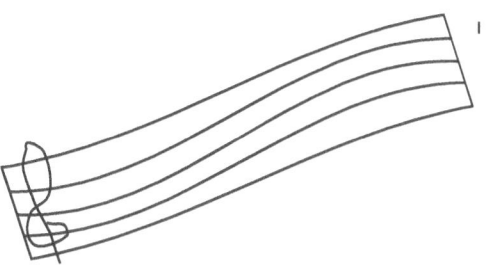

This book belongs to:

_____

If found, please contact me at:

phone: _____

email: _____

Thanks.

ISBN: 978-0-9912927-1-4

New Music Media
(a Division of ProseWorks Media)
Chapel Hill, NC

Address purchase and other inquiries to:
info@proseworks.us

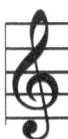

We have all had those wonderful moments of creative inspiration when the Muse mysteriously speaks or sings to us. Hopefully, we jotted the inspired idea down on a scratch piece of paper or, maybe, we had a tape recorder handy - if we can later just find the right tape. In most cases though, we try desperately to remember our brilliant thought until we can "properly" record it later.

But, as often as not, what we remember will not be exactly the same as the unique melody or lyric we had originally conceived. What every songwriter has needed is a book like The *Songwriter's Notebook* - small enough to be easy to carry, big enough not to lose, and formatted so we can quickly and easily record our great ideas, clever lyrics, riffs and melodies that "appear" in that fleeting moment of inspiration.

Use the left hand pages of this book to record lyrics, clever sayings, quotes, poems, conversations and any thing else that might inspire you later. Song titles! Phone numbers of someone you just met who might be a potential accompanist! A pretty scene you came across.

Use the right hand pages to record the musical inspirations you come up with as you move through your day: melodies, base beats, chord sequences...... The page will accommodate notation for piano, guitar, vocals, base guitar and dulcimer and pretty much anything else.

Carry The *Songwriter's Notebook* with you everywhere to record and never again lose those fleeting and inspirational communications you receive from your Muse.

Song name: My Baby - Mar 24

My baby done left me
She done ~~gone~~ and run
I'll miss her to pieces
But I will have some fun

My baby done left me
She left me for ~~good~~ John   good
~~I know I should chase her~~
~~I know that I should.~~

Great Image: red sky at sunset,
girl walking by with purple
shoes and a white hat....lovely
on Spring Street

Alas for those that never sing,
But die with all their music in them!
~Oliver Wendell Holmes

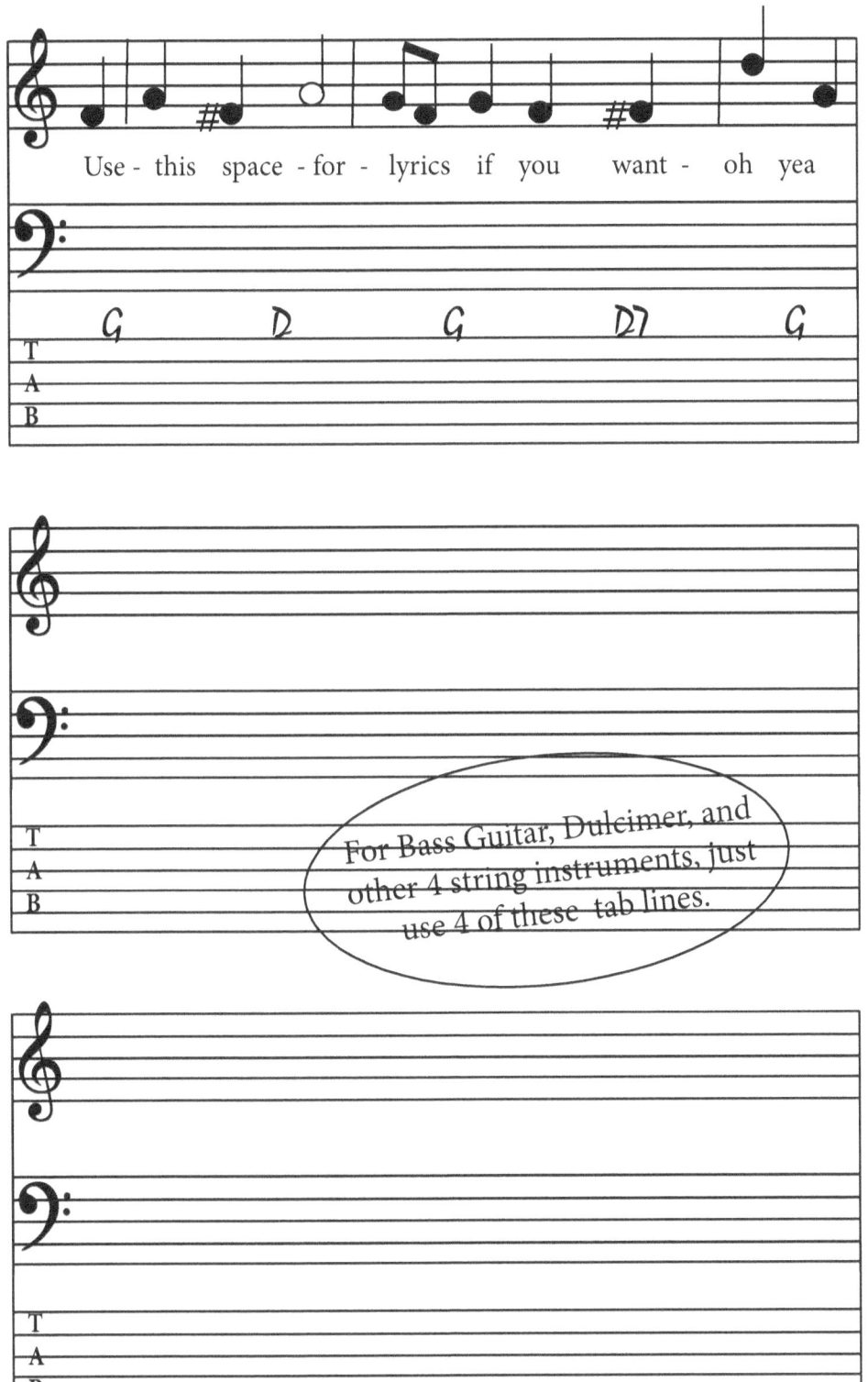

Use - this space - for - lyrics if you want - oh yea

G   D   G   D7   G

For Bass Guitar, Dulcimer, and other 4 string instruments, just use 4 of these tab lines.

Take a music bath once or twice a week for a few seasons. You will
find it is to the soul what a water bath is to the body.
~Oliver Wendell Holmes

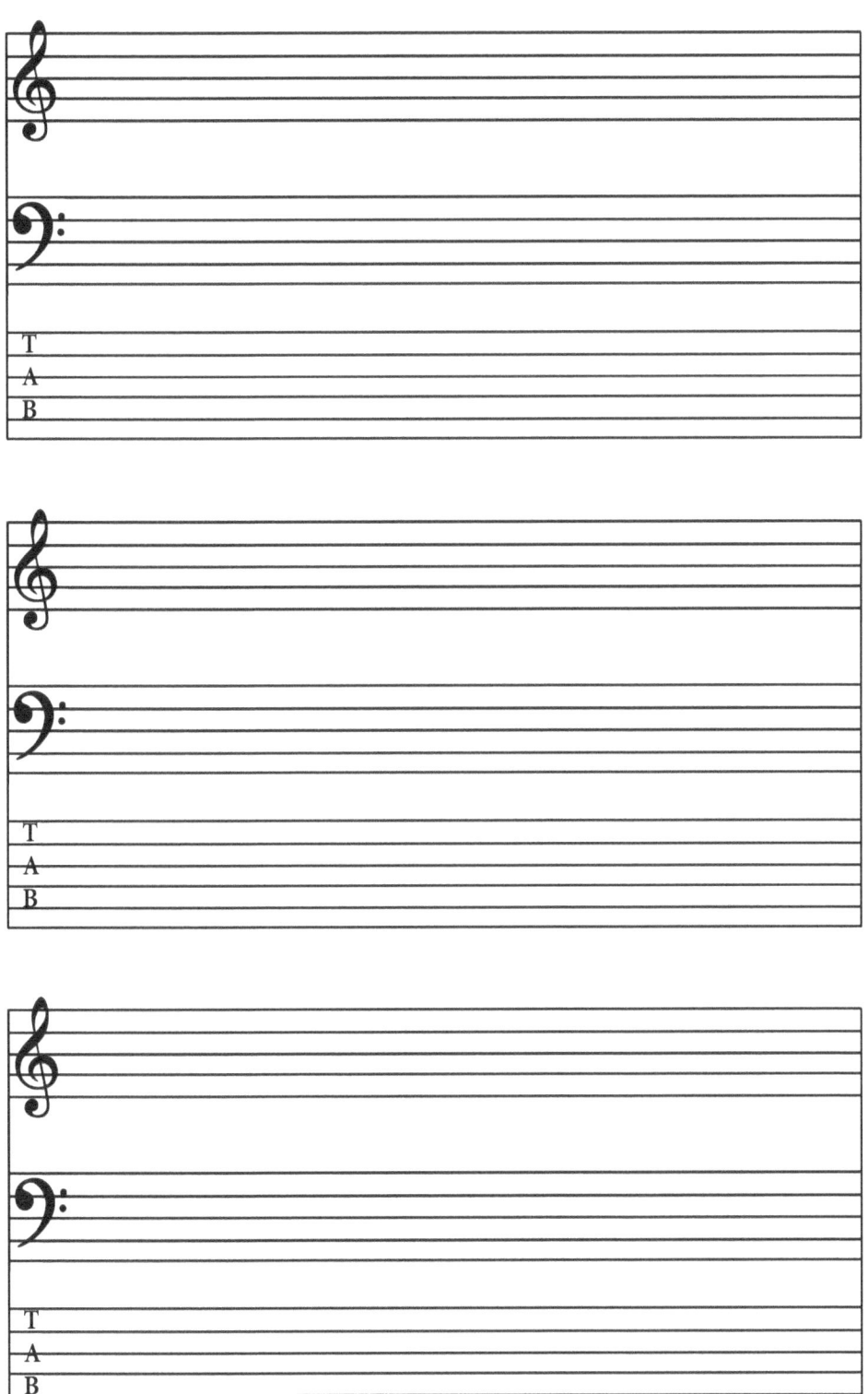

Music is your own experience, your thoughts, your wisdom. If you don't live it, it won't come out of your horn.
~Charlie Parker

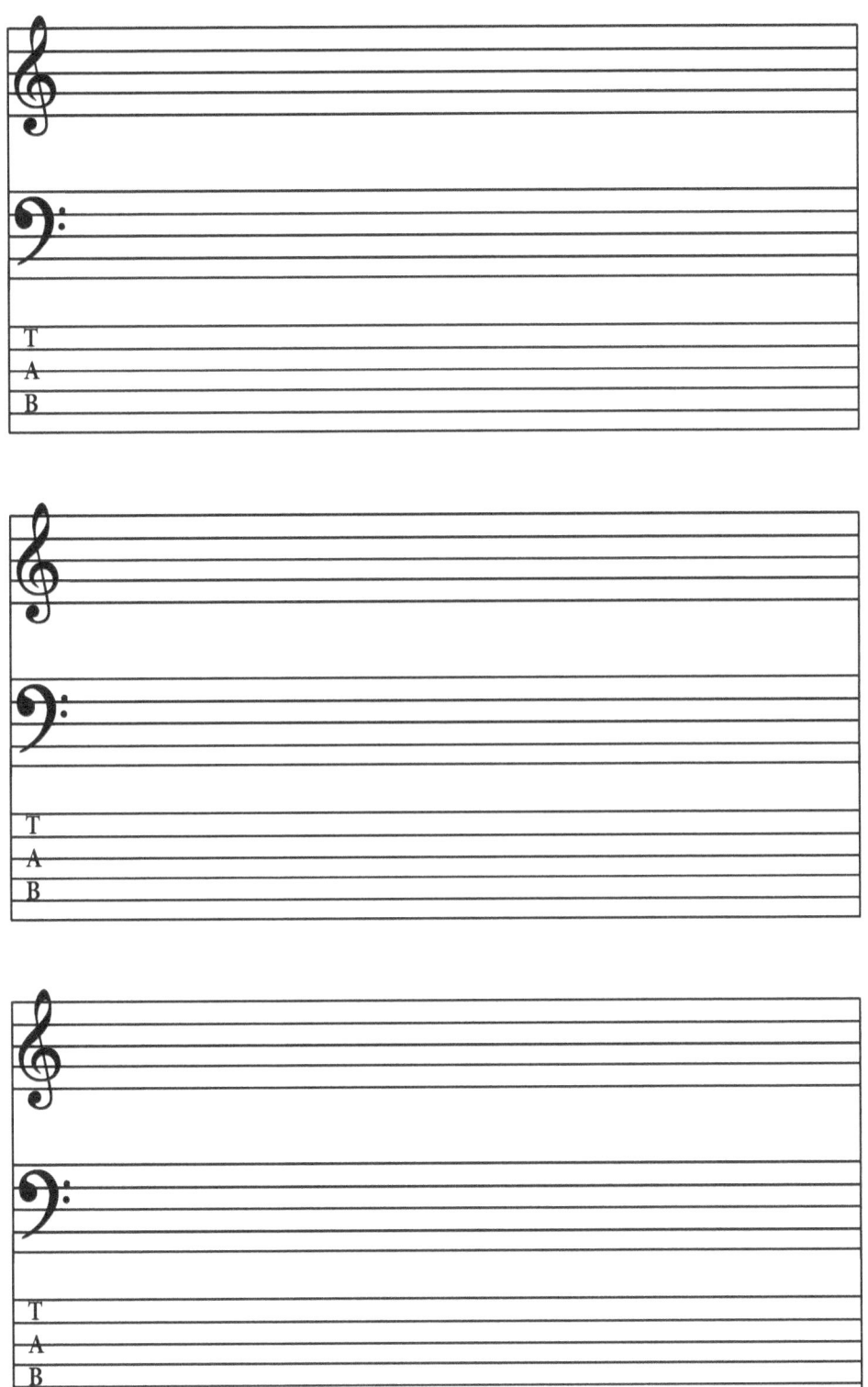

Music is the universal language of mankind.
~Henry Wadsworth Longfellow, *Outre-Mer*

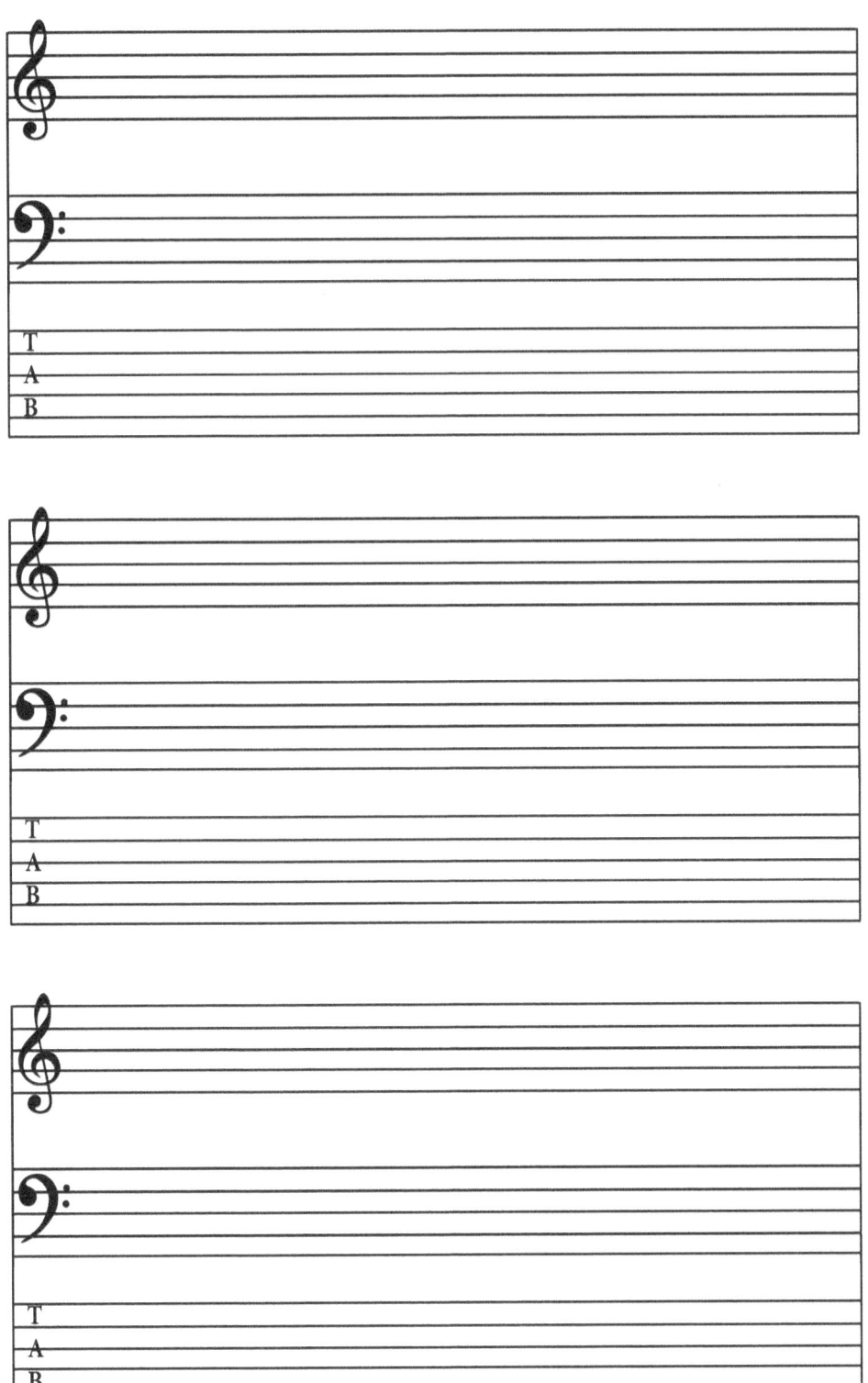

Music is what life sounds like.
~Eric Olson

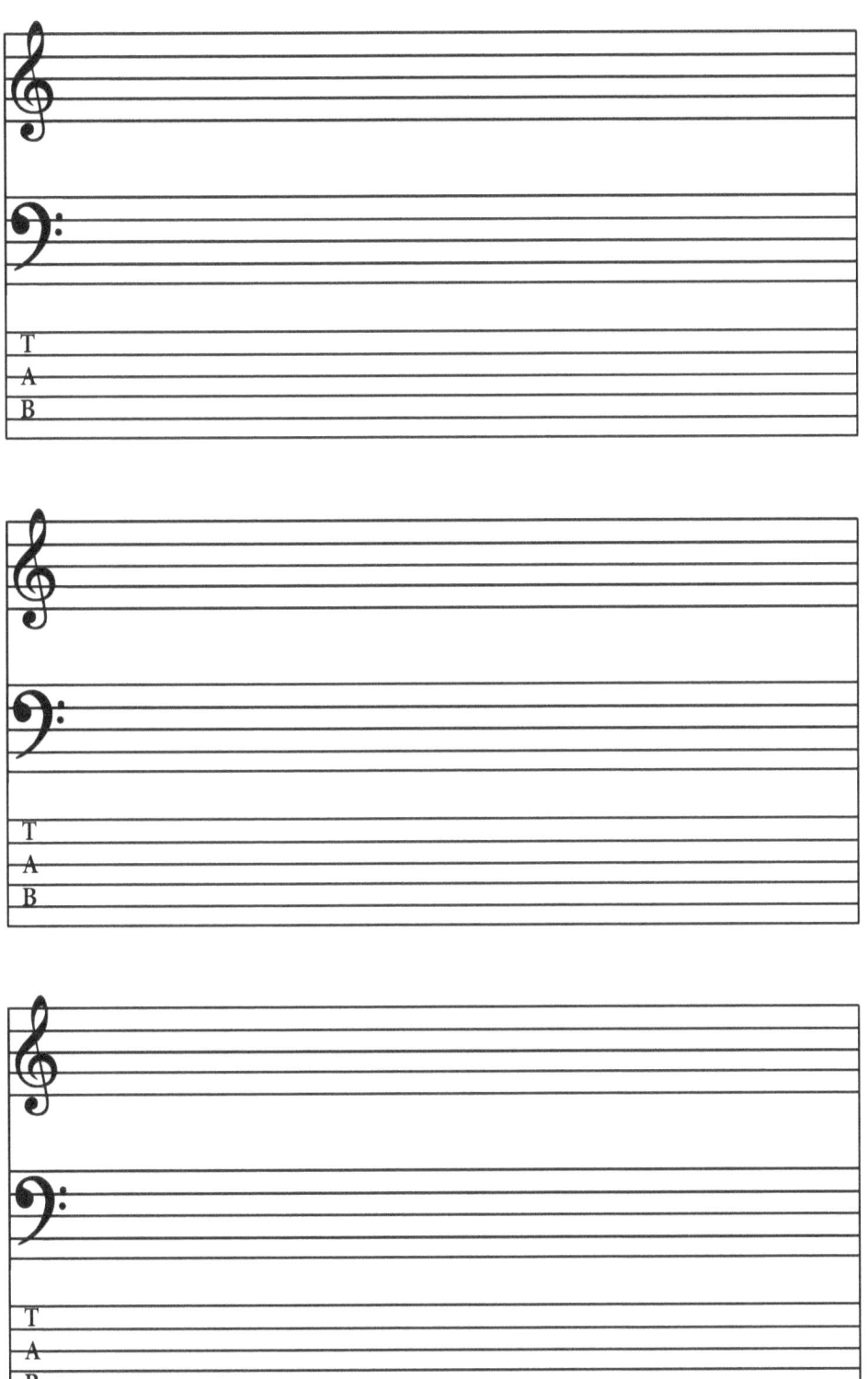

Music is a higher revelation than all wisdom and philosophy.
~Ludwig van Beethoven

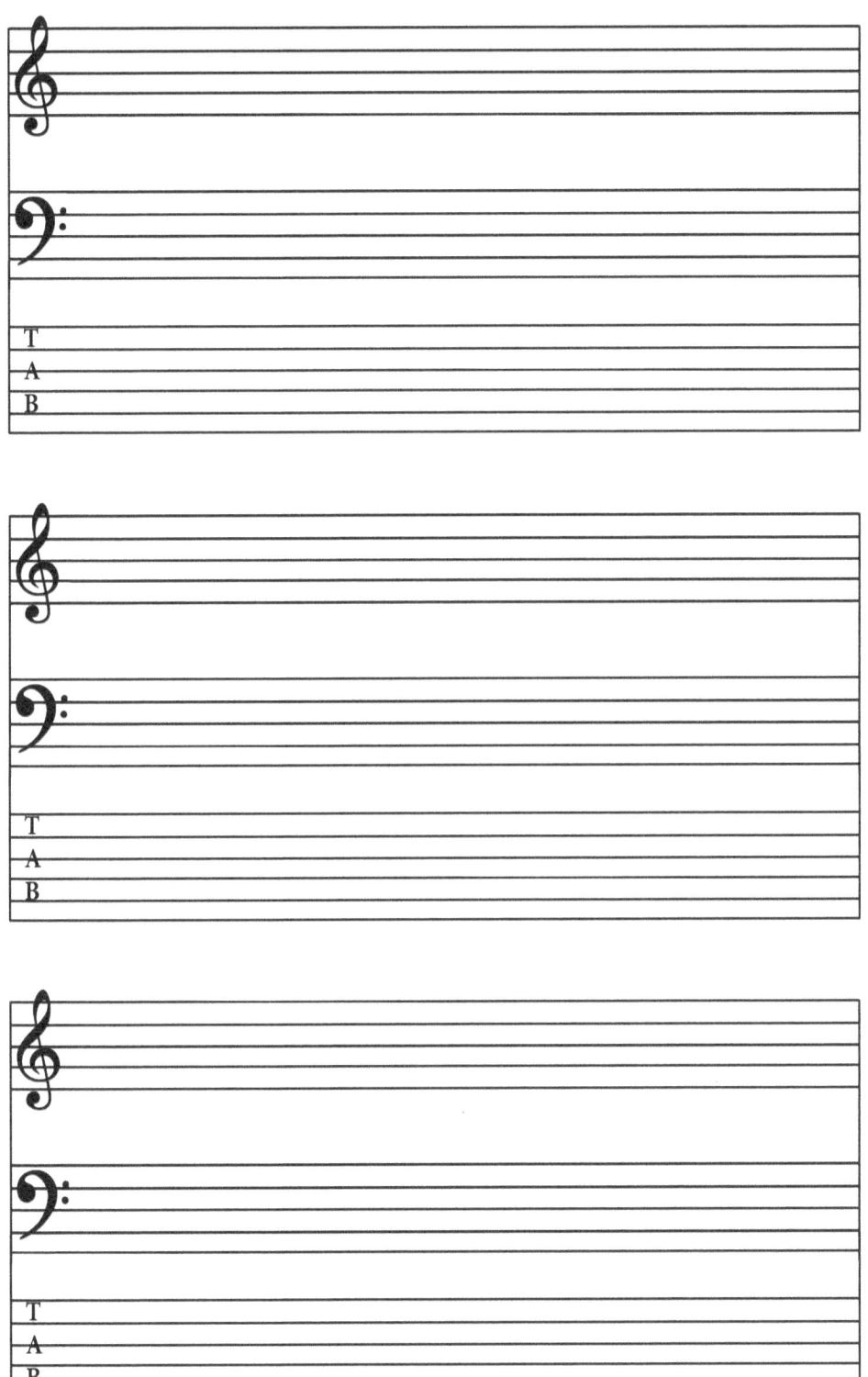

I write music with an exclamation point!
-Richard Wagner

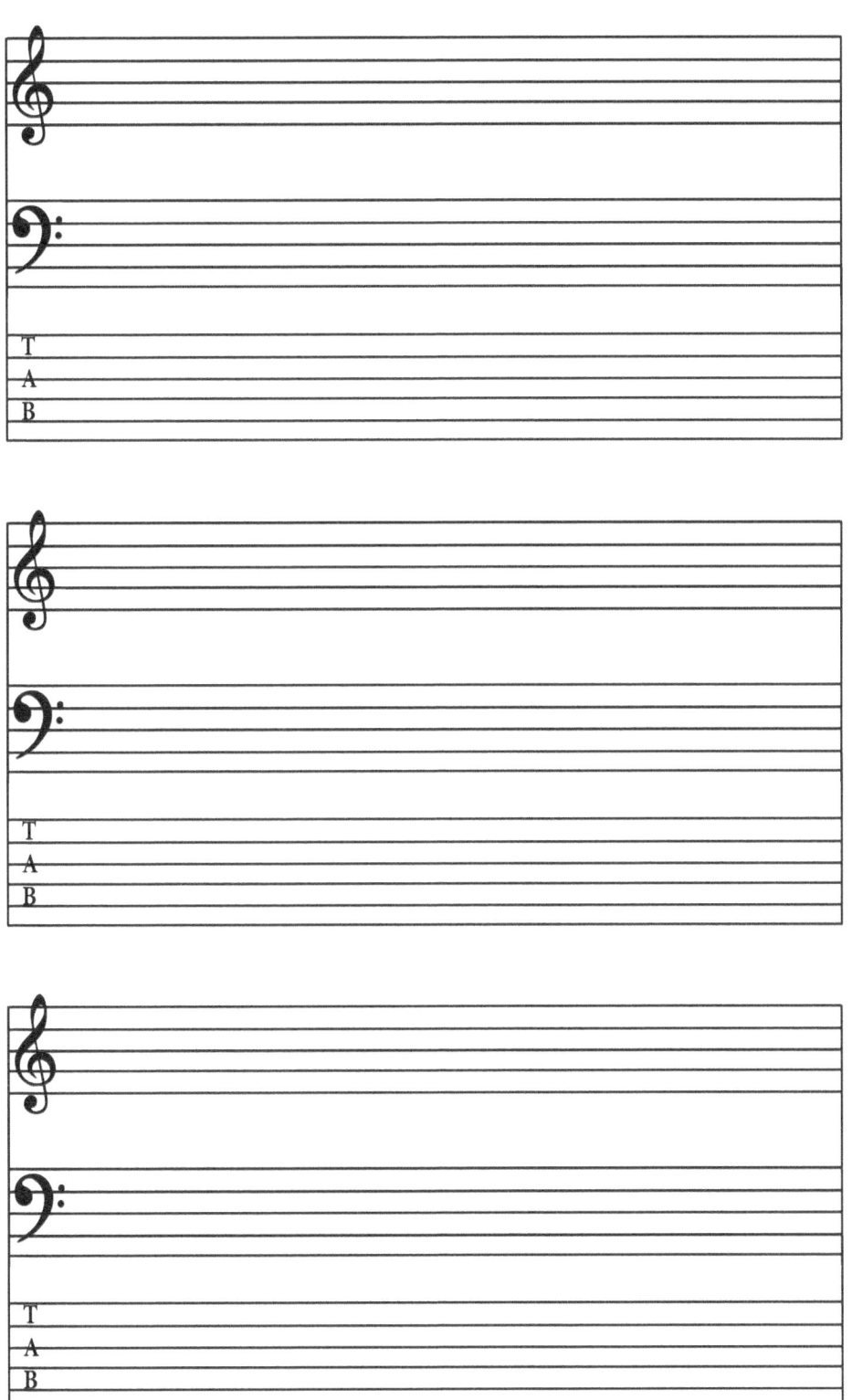

Music can change the world because it can change people.
-Bono, U2

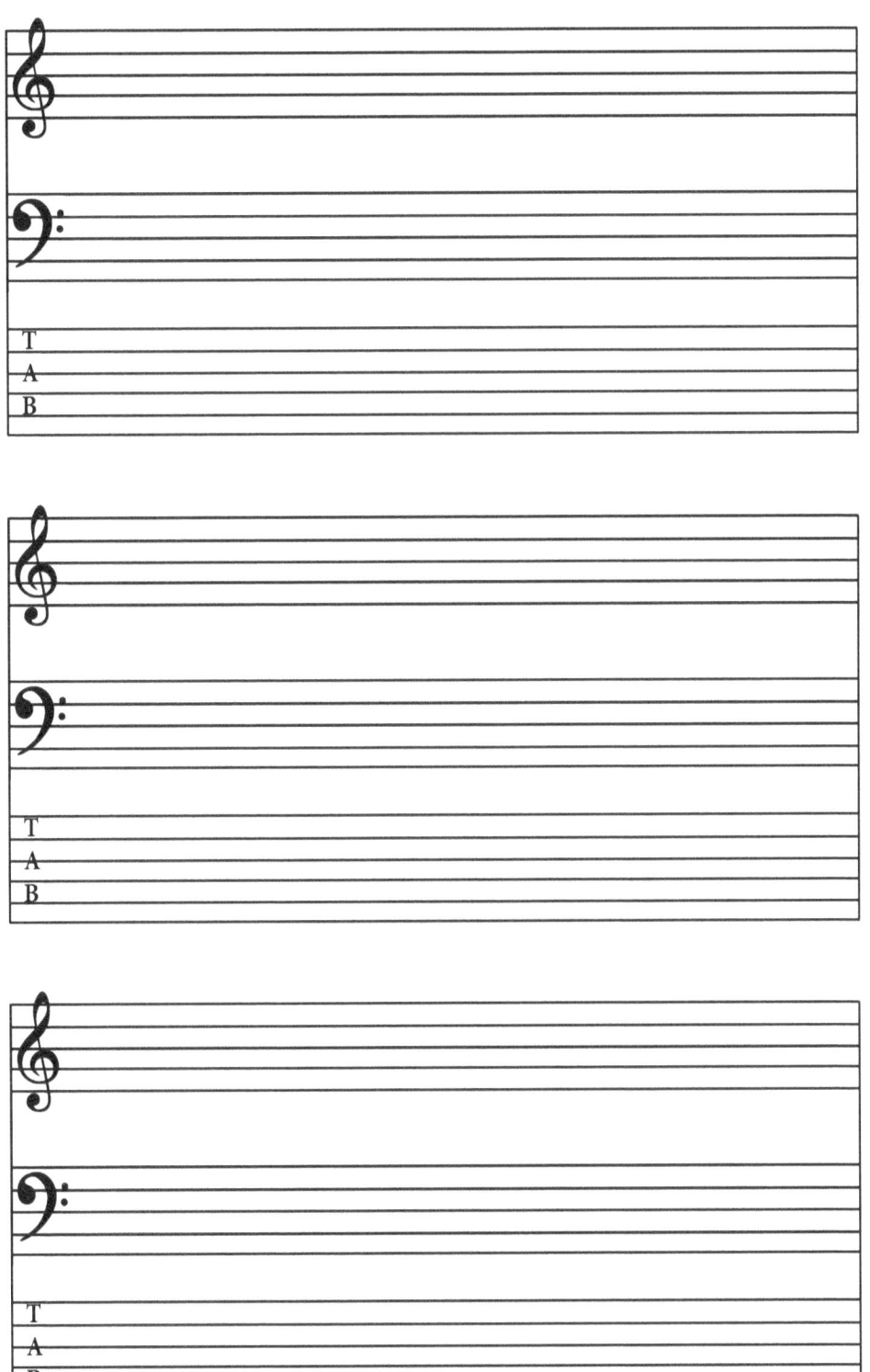

Music expresses that which cannot be said and
on which it is impossible to be silent.
~Victor Hugo

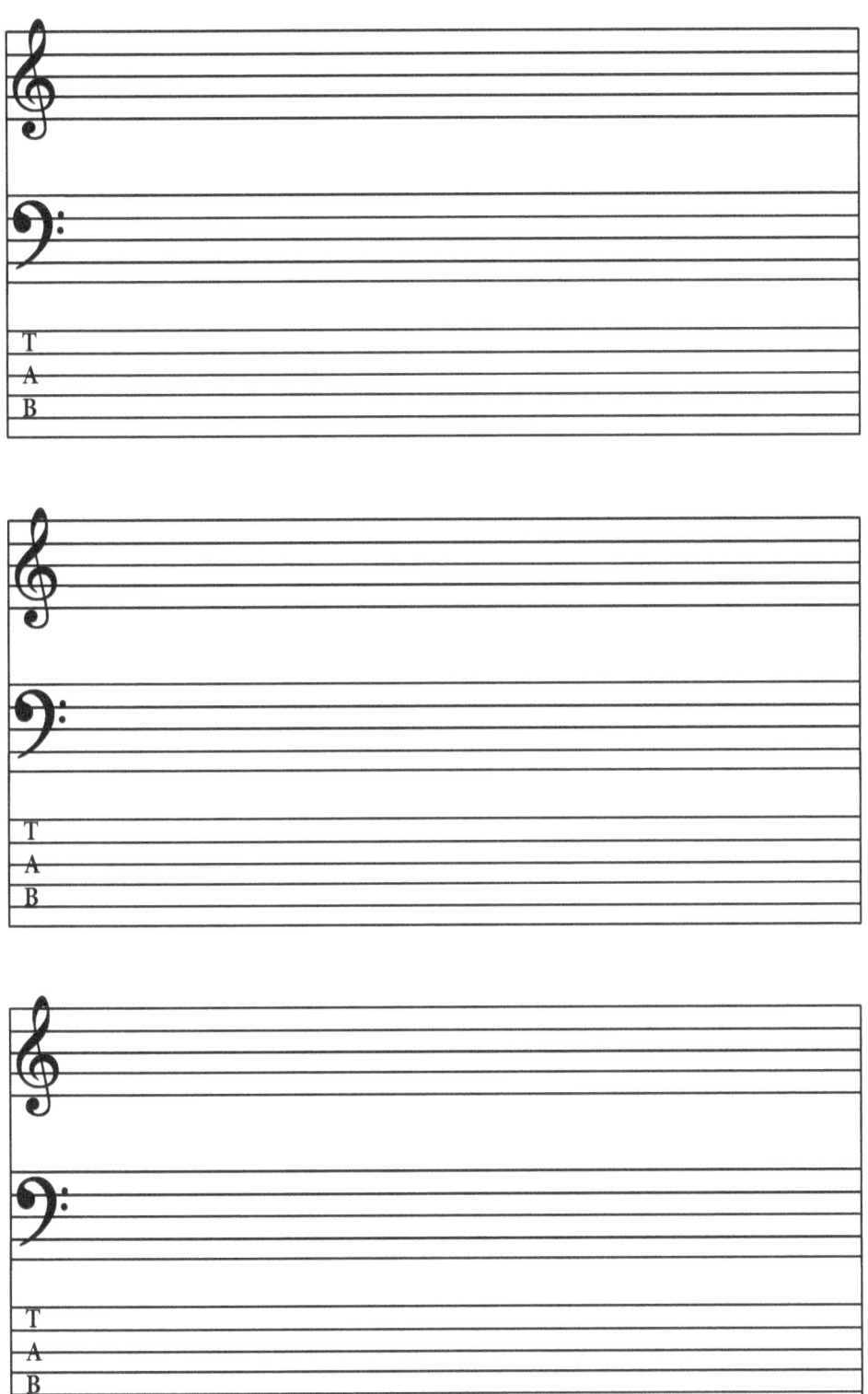

All music is folk music. I ain't never heard a horse sing a song.
~Louis Armstrong

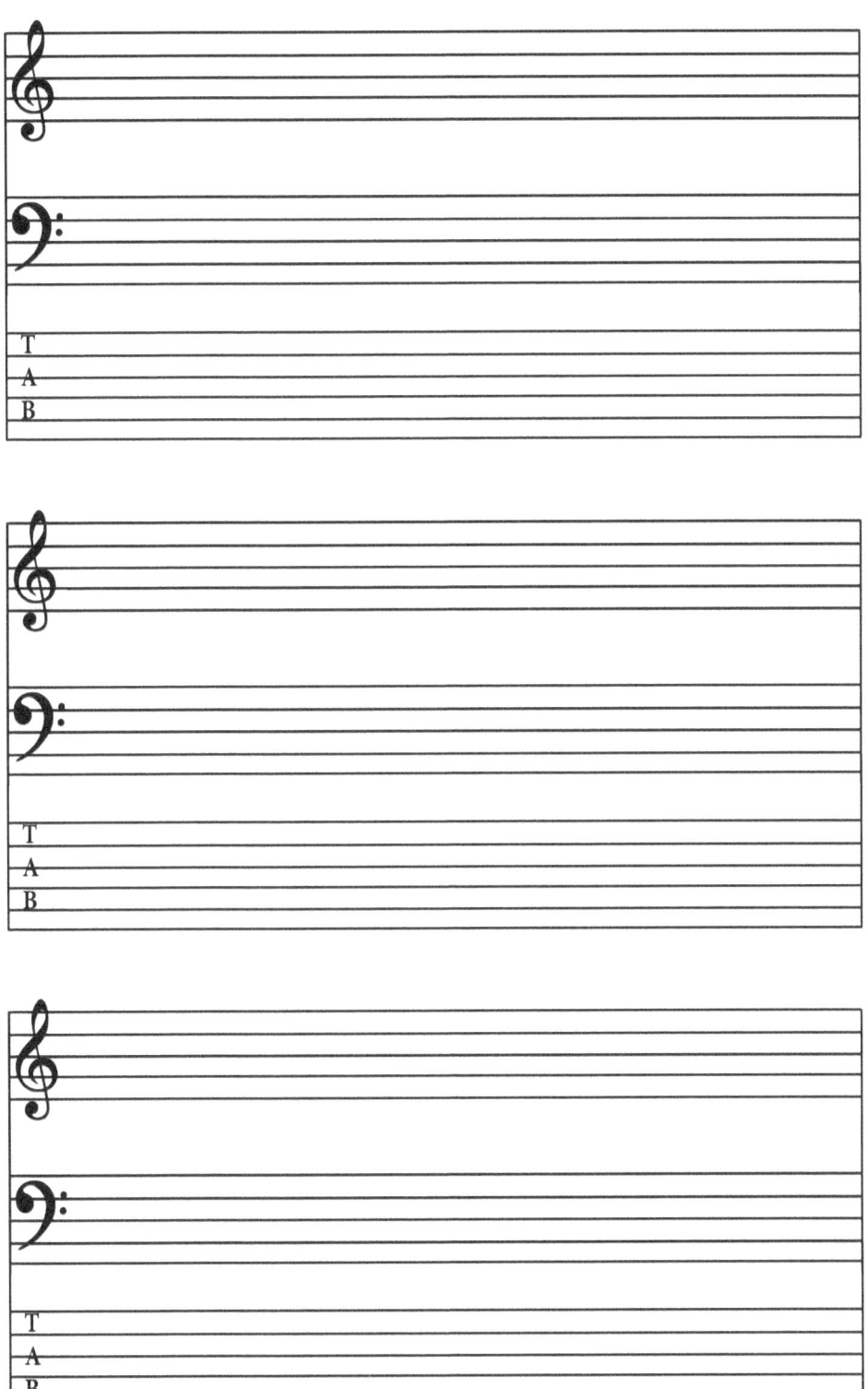

What passion cannot music raise and quell!
~John Dryden

The notes I handle no better than many pianists. But the pauses
between the notes - ah, that is where the art resides!
~Artur Schnabel

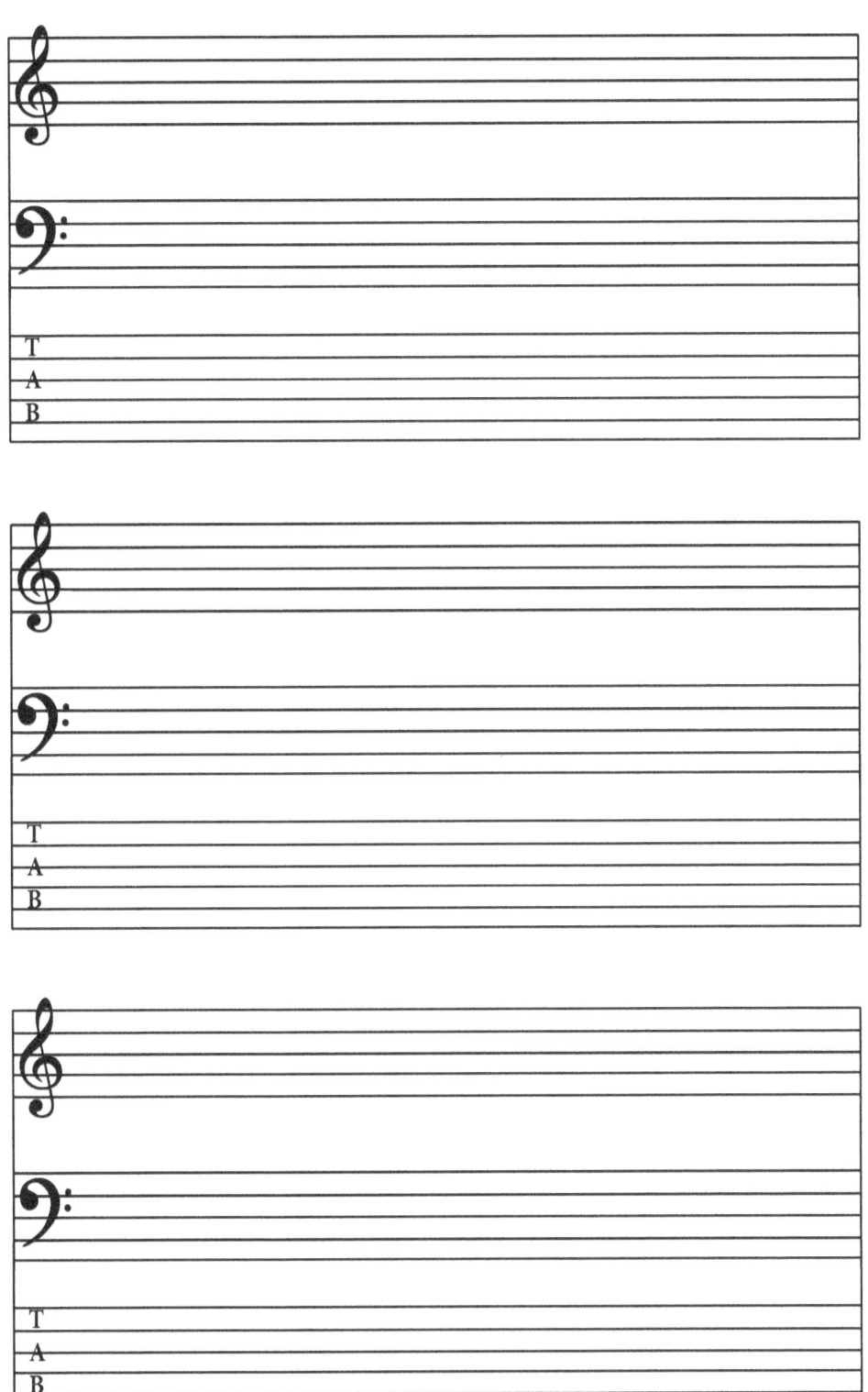

My whole trick is to keep the tune well out in front. If I play Tchai-kovsky, I play his melodies and skip his spiritual struggle.
~Liberace

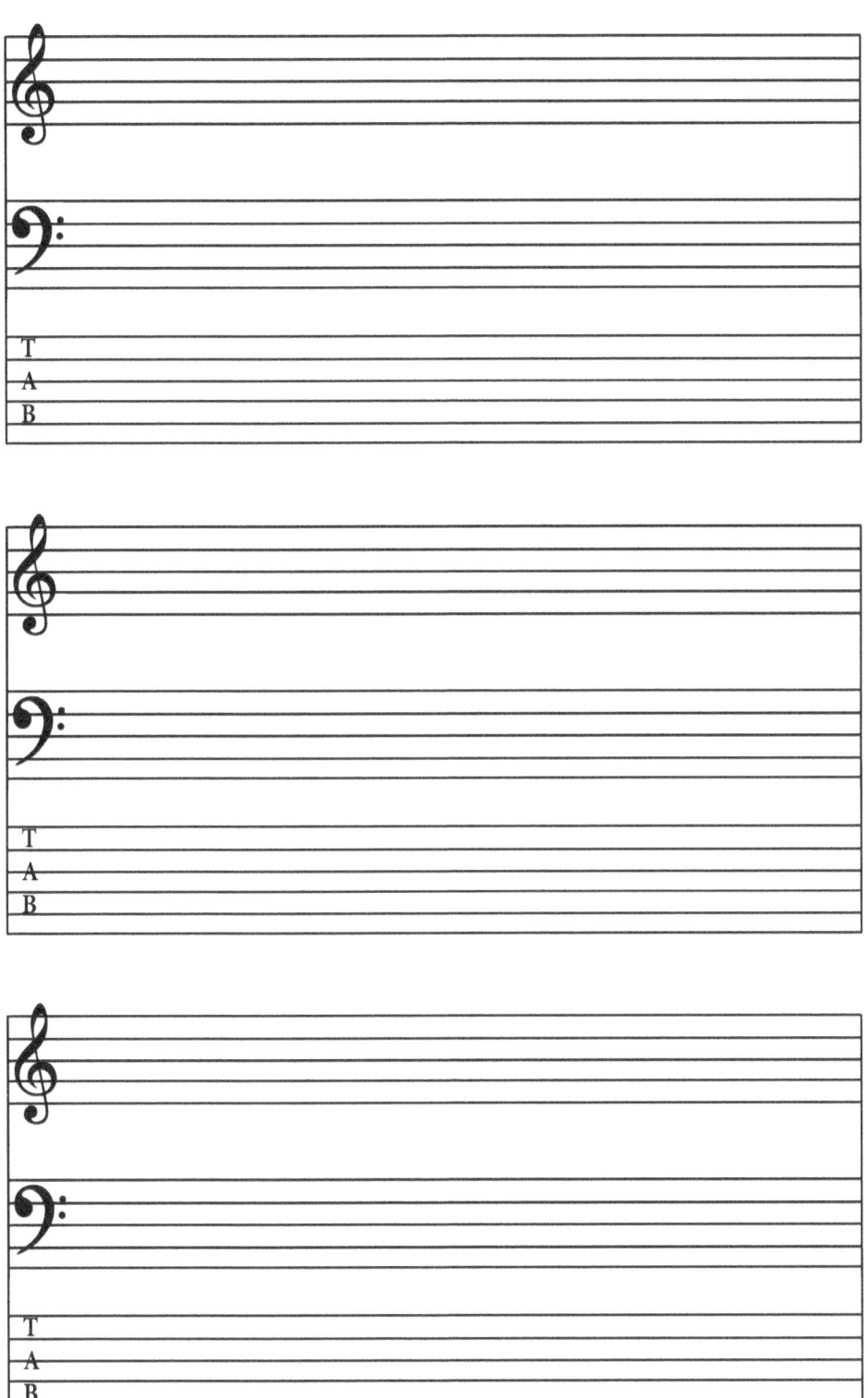

A bird does not sing because it has an answer.
It sings because it has a song.
-Chinese Proverb

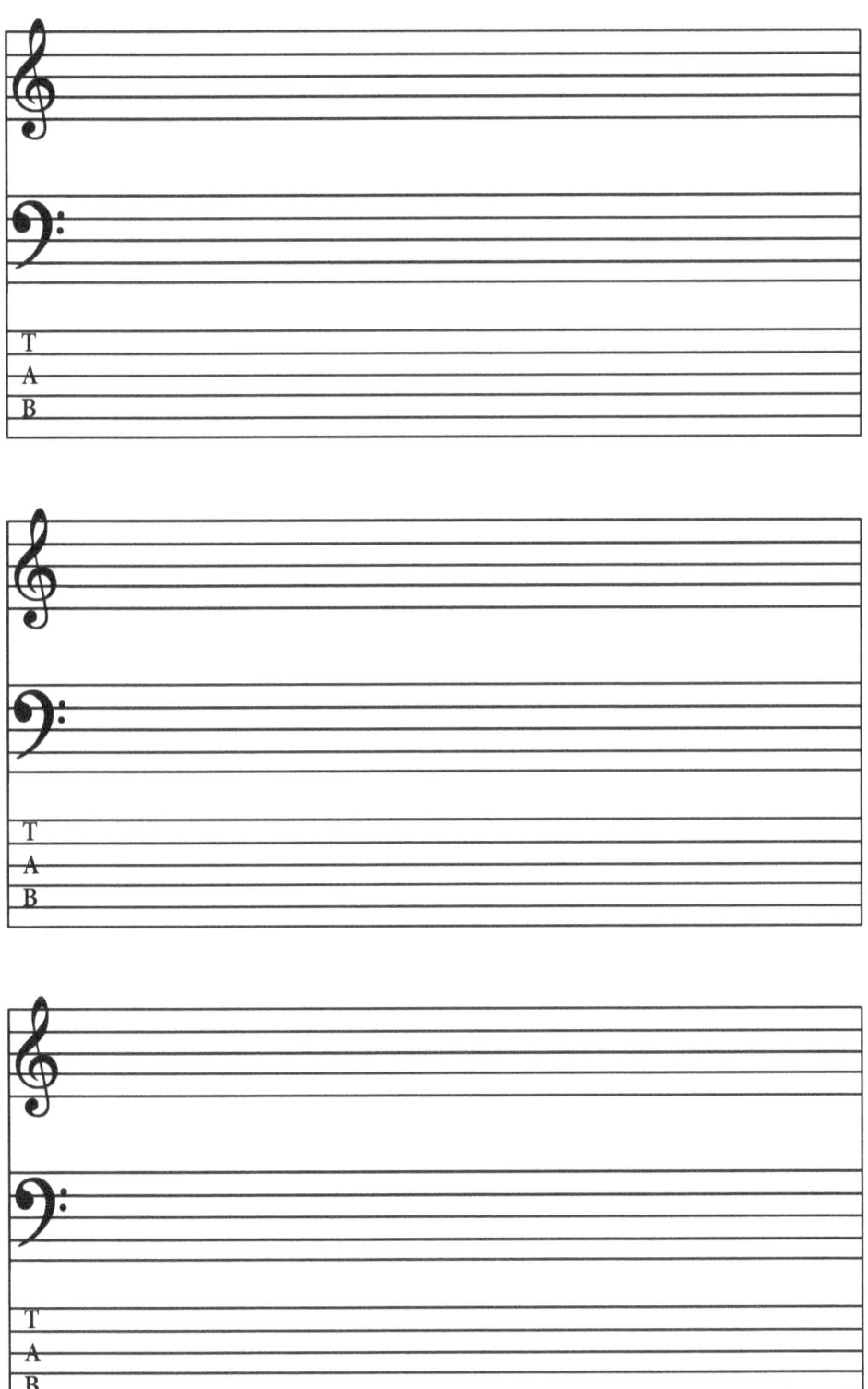

Opera is where a guy gets stabbed in the back, and
instead of dying, he sings.
~Robert Benchley

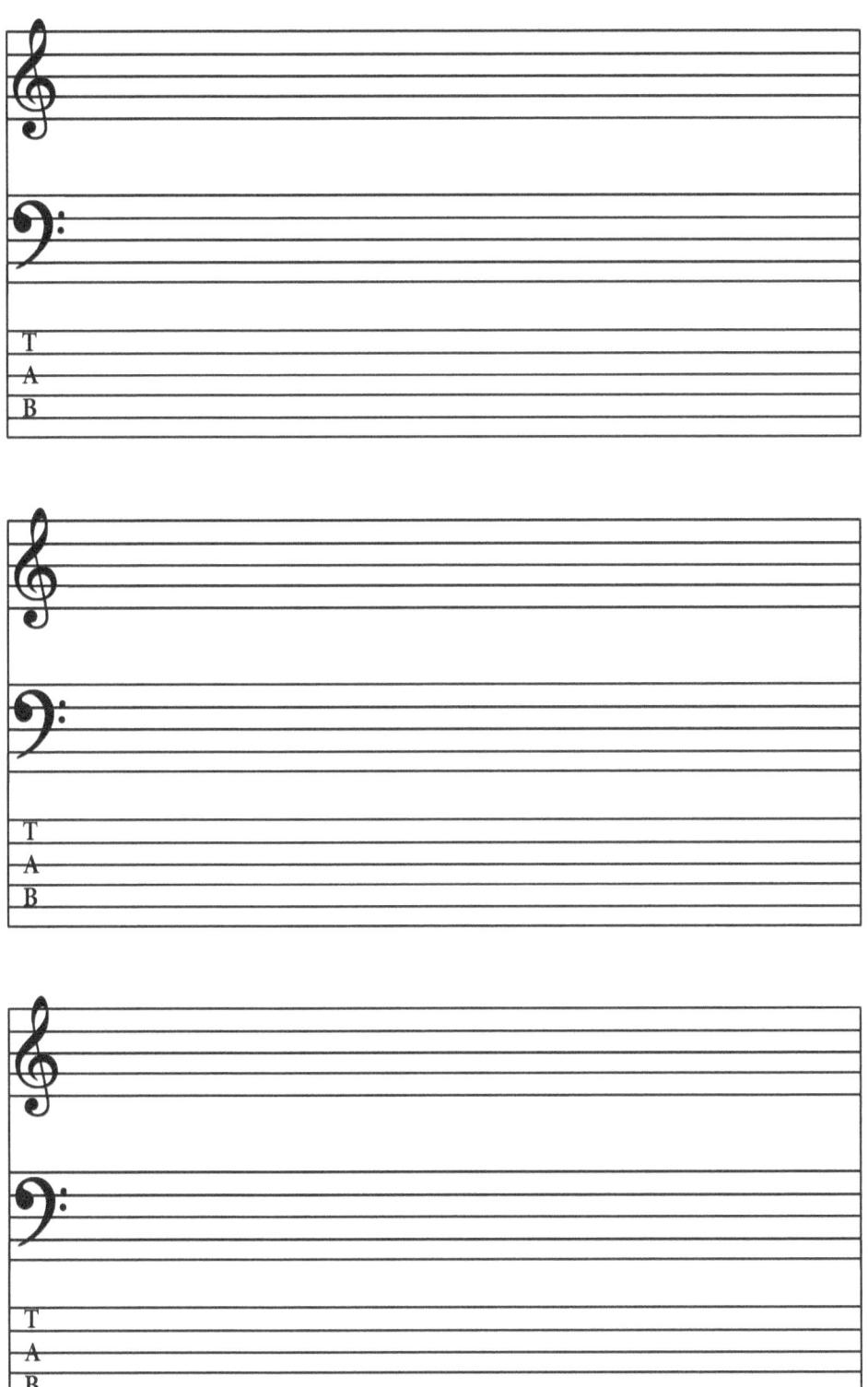

Creativity is more than just being different. Anybody can plan weird; that's easy. What's hard is to be as simple as Bach. Making the simple, awesomely simple, that's creativity. ~Charles Mingus

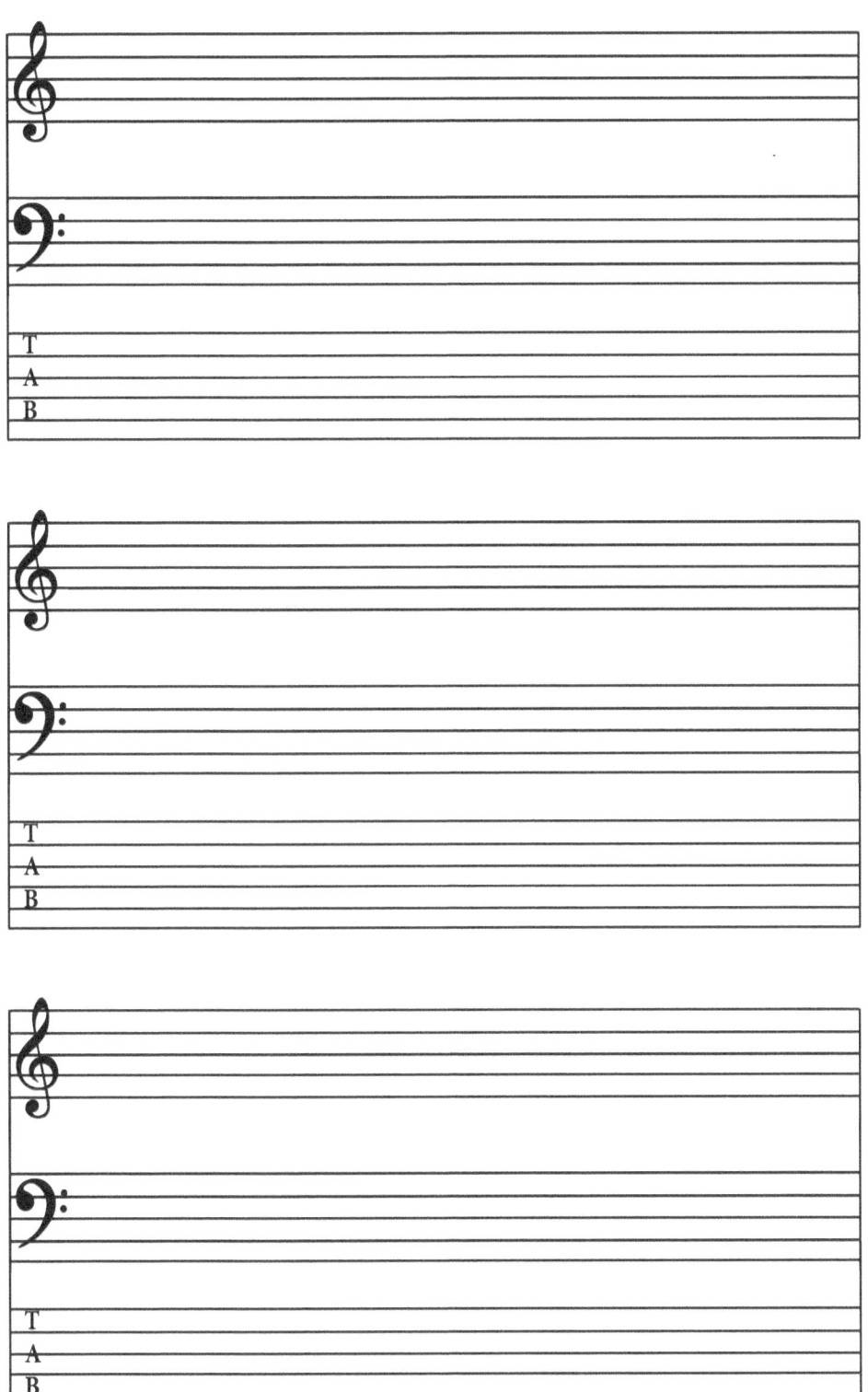

Creativity - like human life itself - begins in darkness.
~Julia Cameron

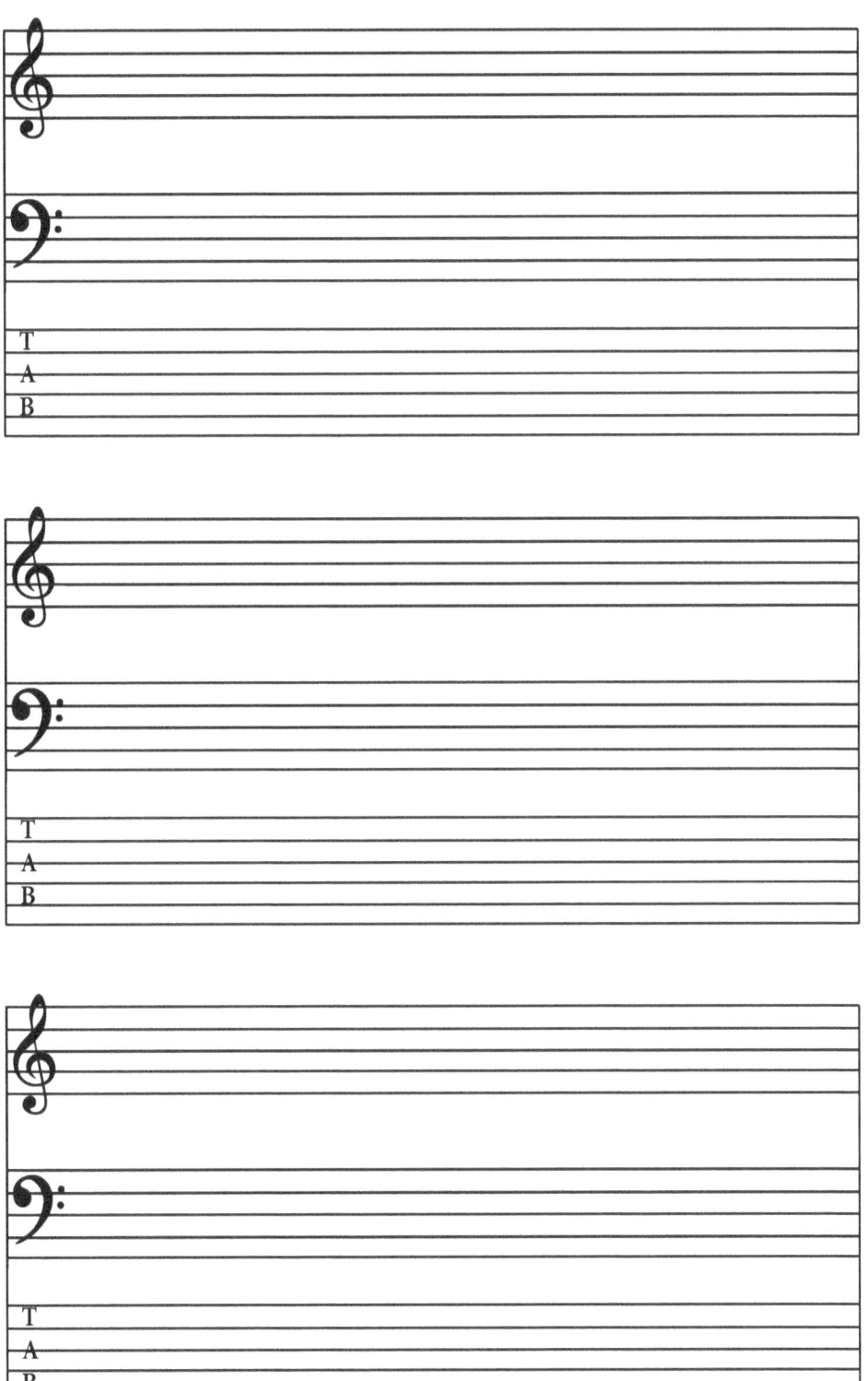

Have no fear of perfection, you'll never reach it.
~Salvador Dali

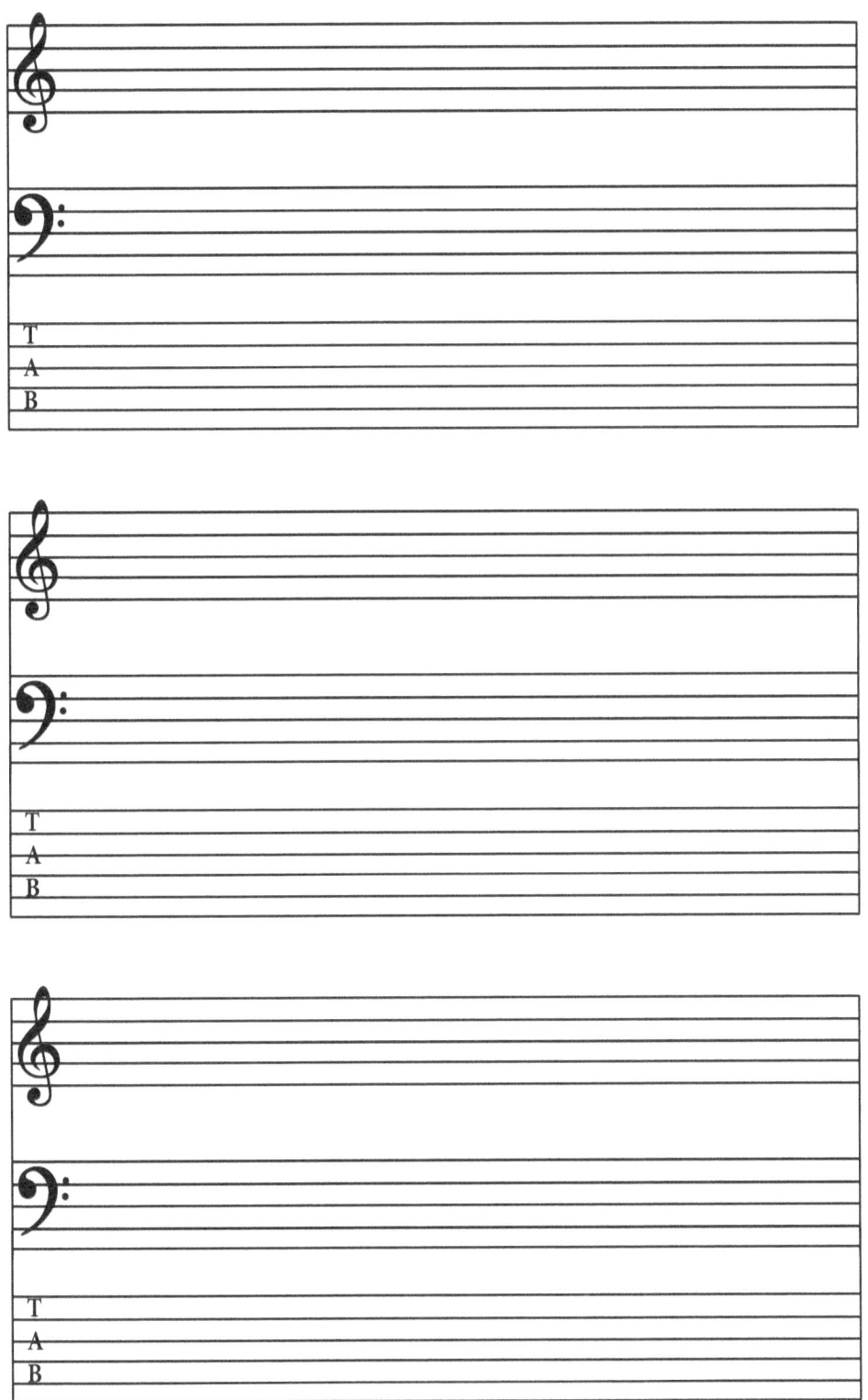

Learning to read music in Braille and play by ear helped me develop a damn good memory.
~Ray Charles

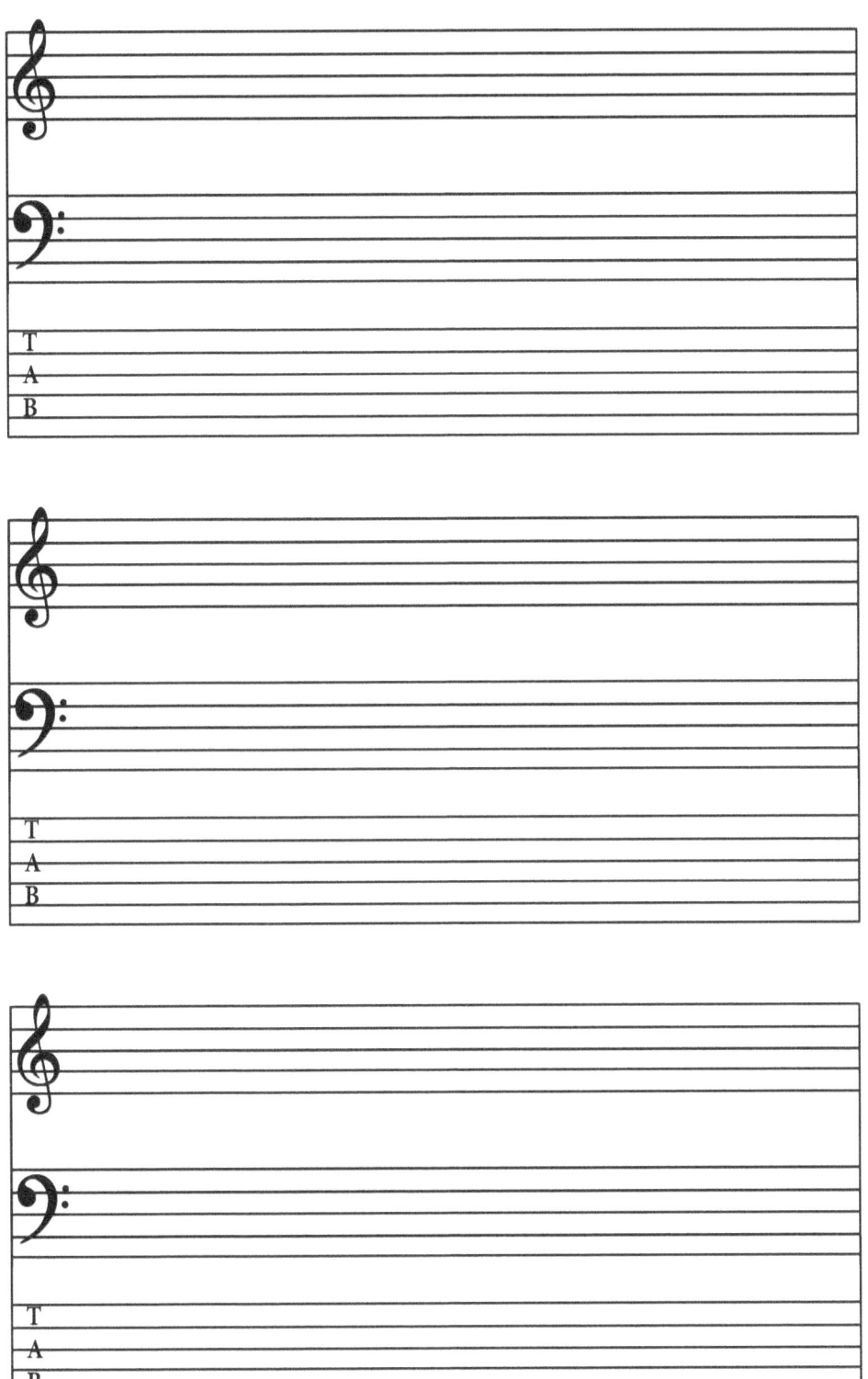

Creativity comes from trust. Trust your instincts.
~Rita Mae Brown

In order to compose, all you need to do is remember a tune that nobody else has thought of.
~Robert Schumann

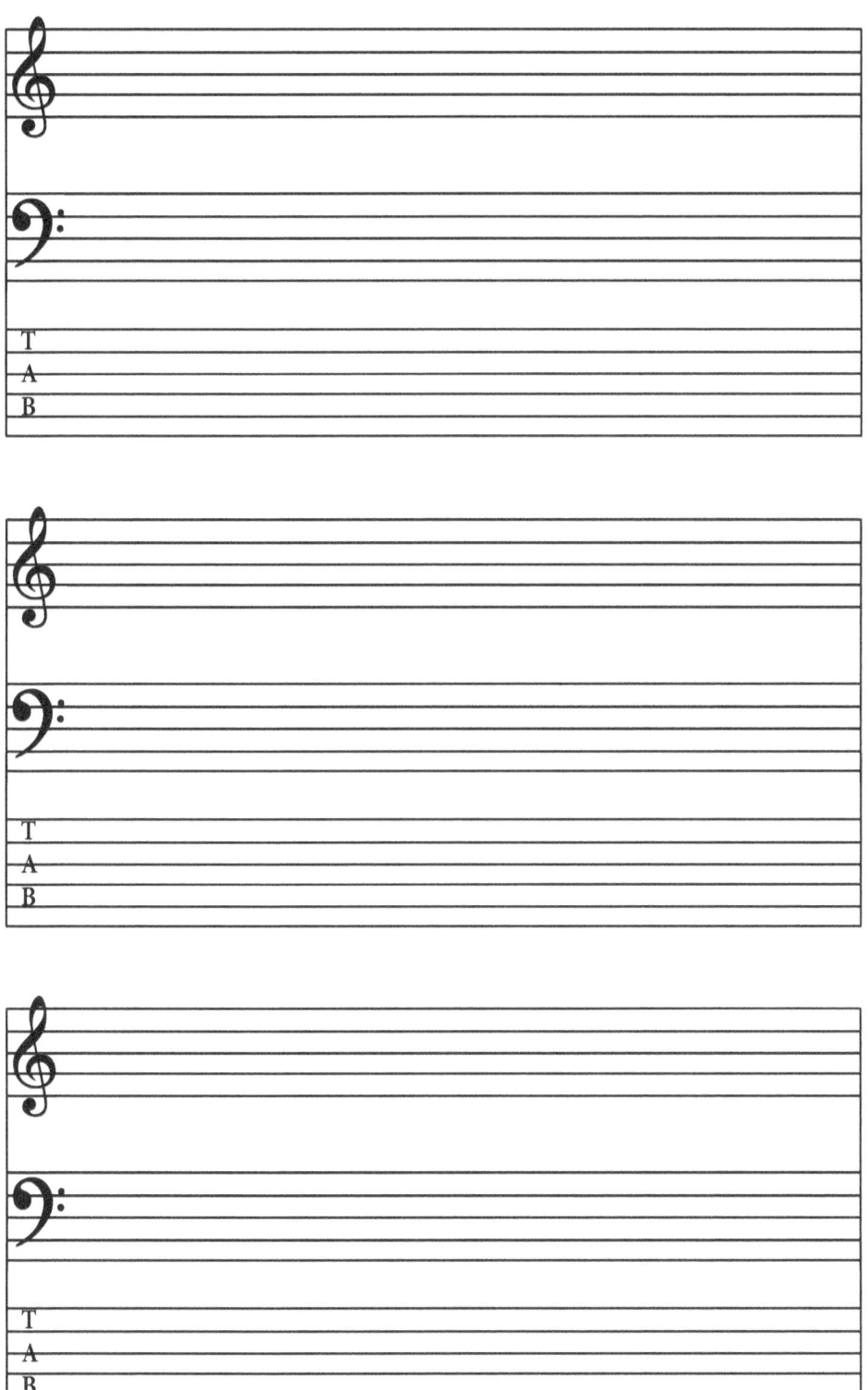

My driving philosophy about making music is that you can reduce it all down to one note if that note is played with the right kind of sincerity.
~Eric Clapton

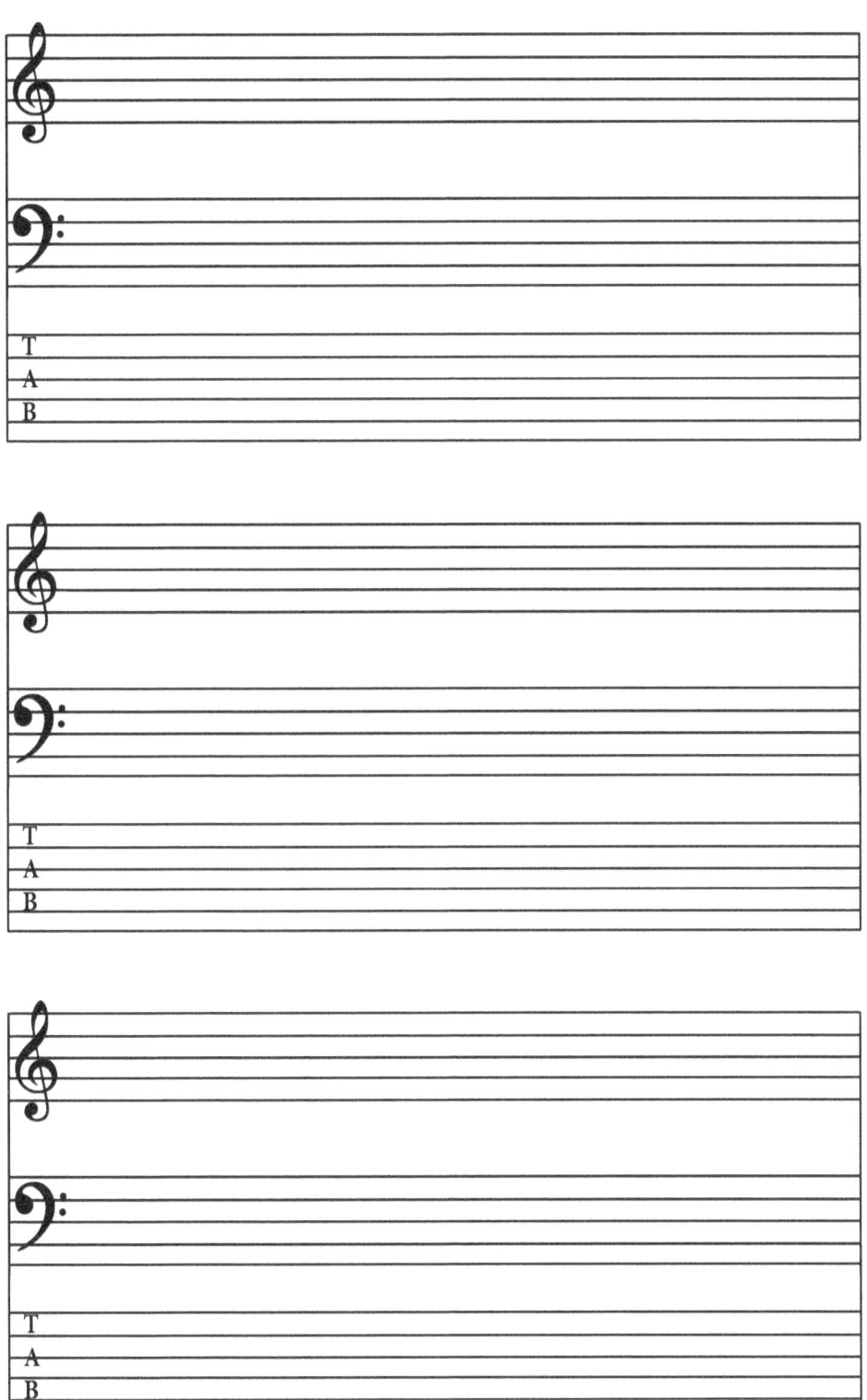

Time you enjoy wasting was not wasted.
~John Lennon

Music should never be harmless.
~Robbie Robertson

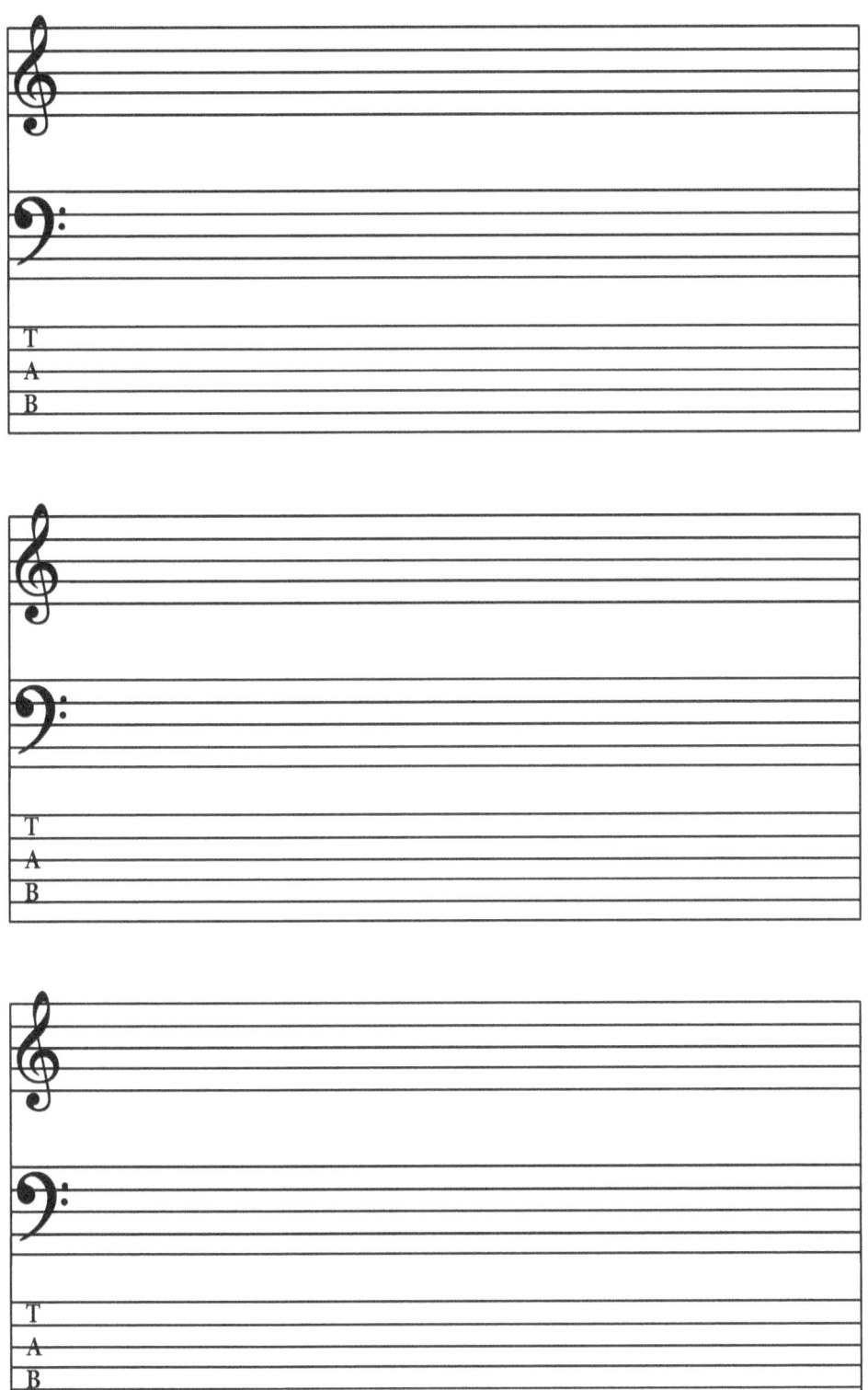

The one thing that can solve most of our problems is dancing...
~James Brown

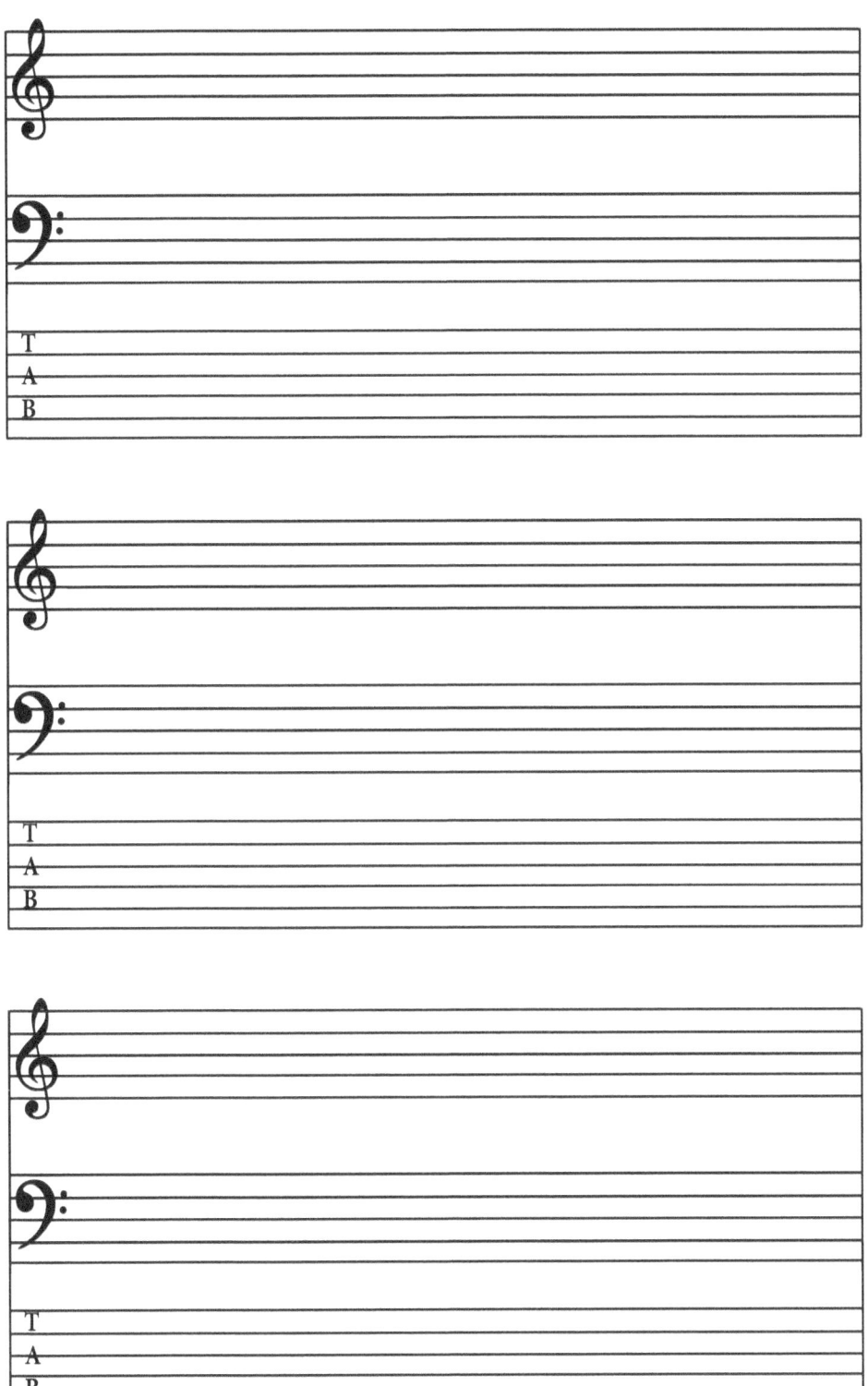

Technically, I am not a guitar player, all I play is truth and emotion.
~Jimi Hendrix

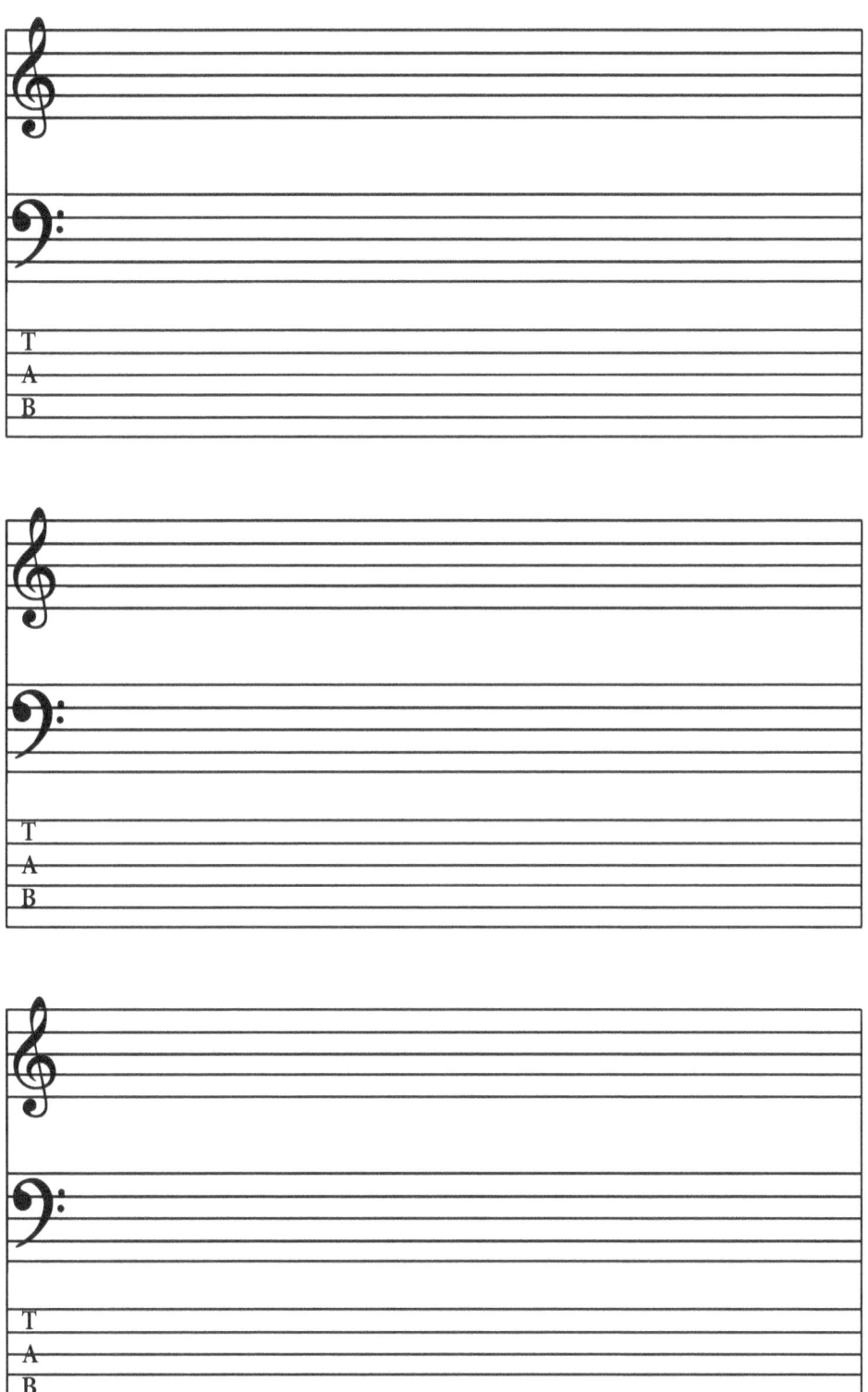

The pause is as important as the note.
~Truman R. Fisher (composer)

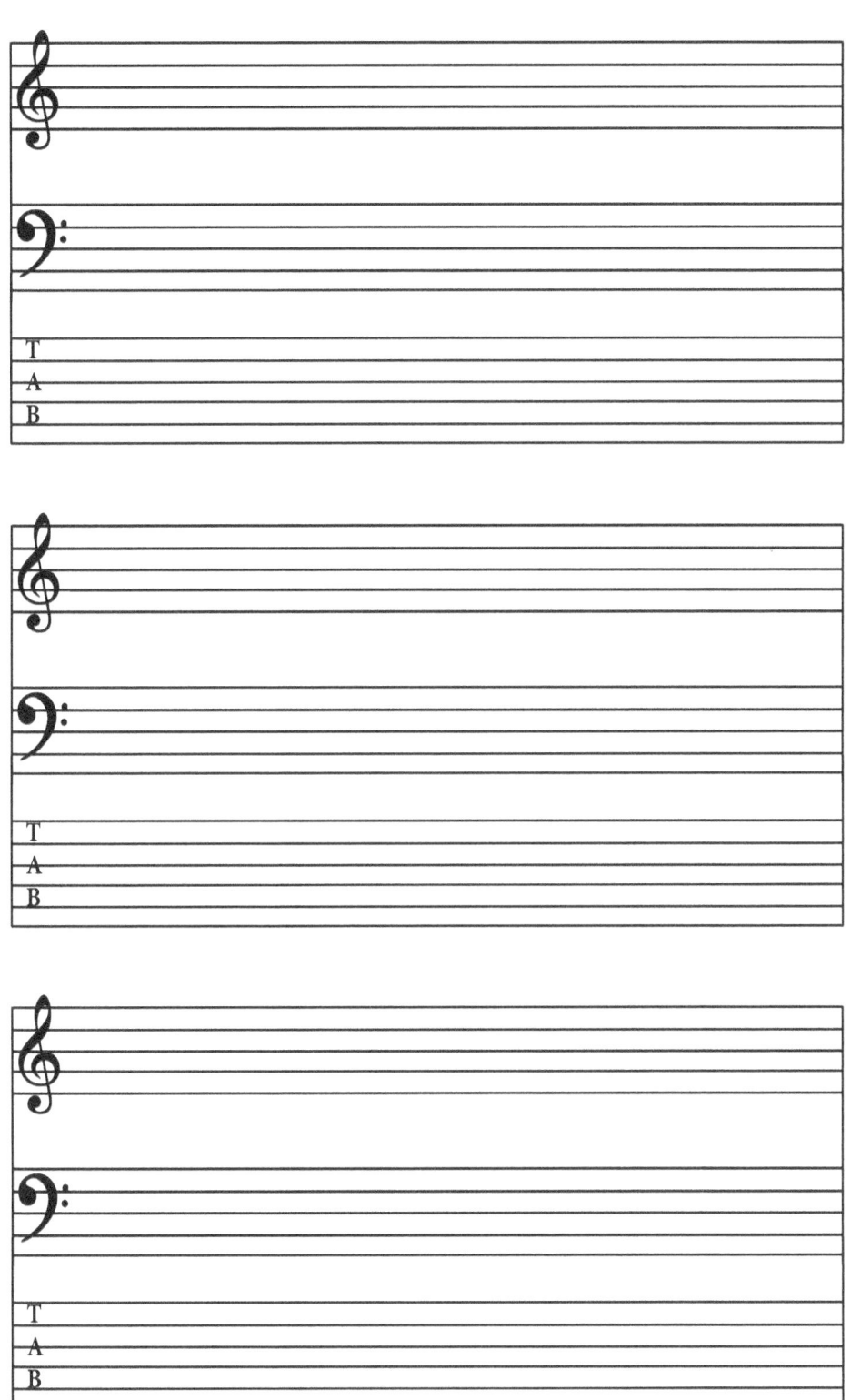

I don't know anything about music. In my line you don't have to.
~Elvis Presley (1935 - 1977)

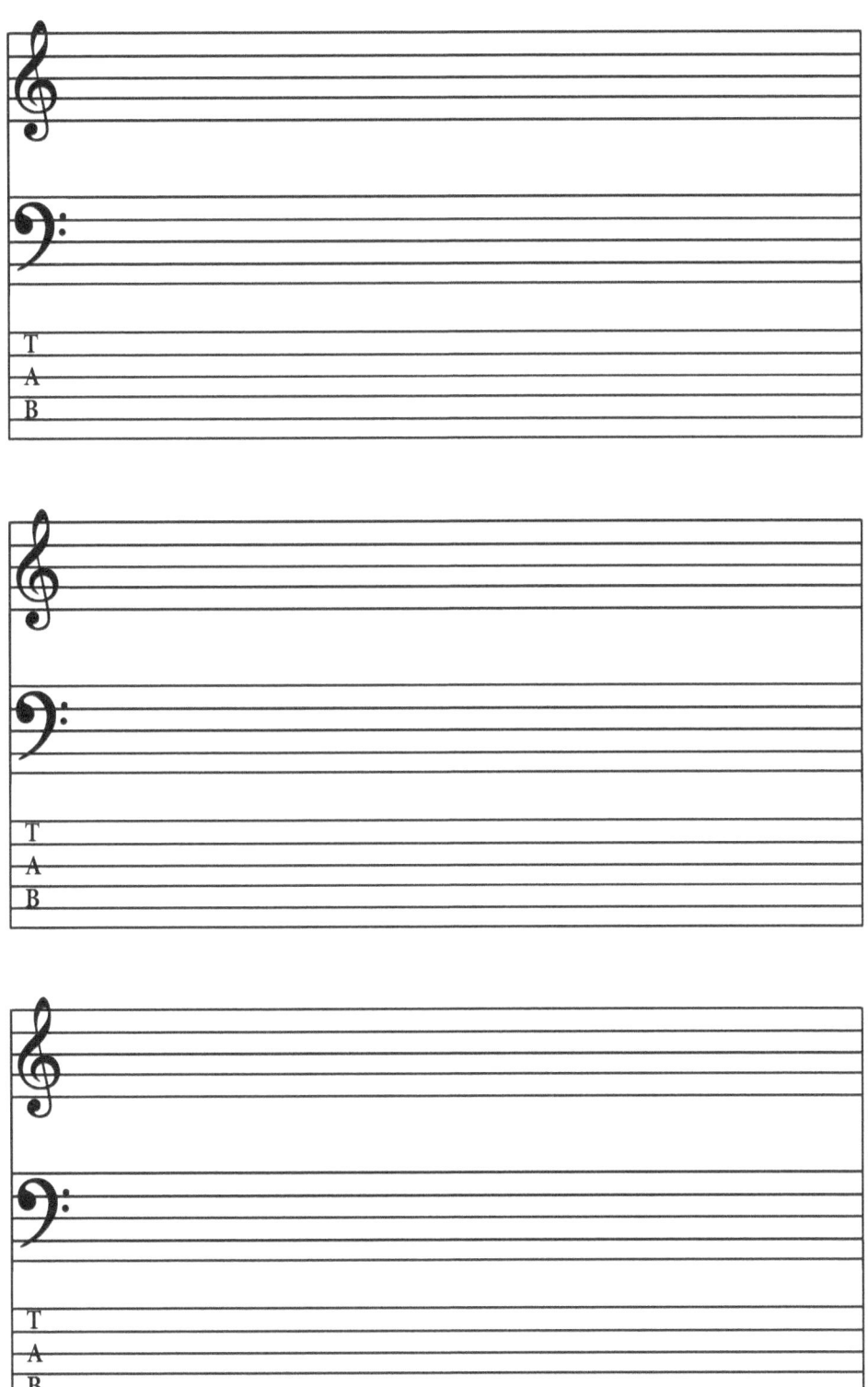

Music has charms to soothe the savage breast
To soften rocks, or bend a knotted oak.
~William Congreve (1670 - 1729), The Mourning Bride, Act 1 Scene 1

There are still so many beautiful things to be said in C Major.
~Sergei Prokofiev

You can't possibly hear the last movement of Beethoven's Seventh and go slow.
~Oscar Levant, explaining his way out of a speeding ticket

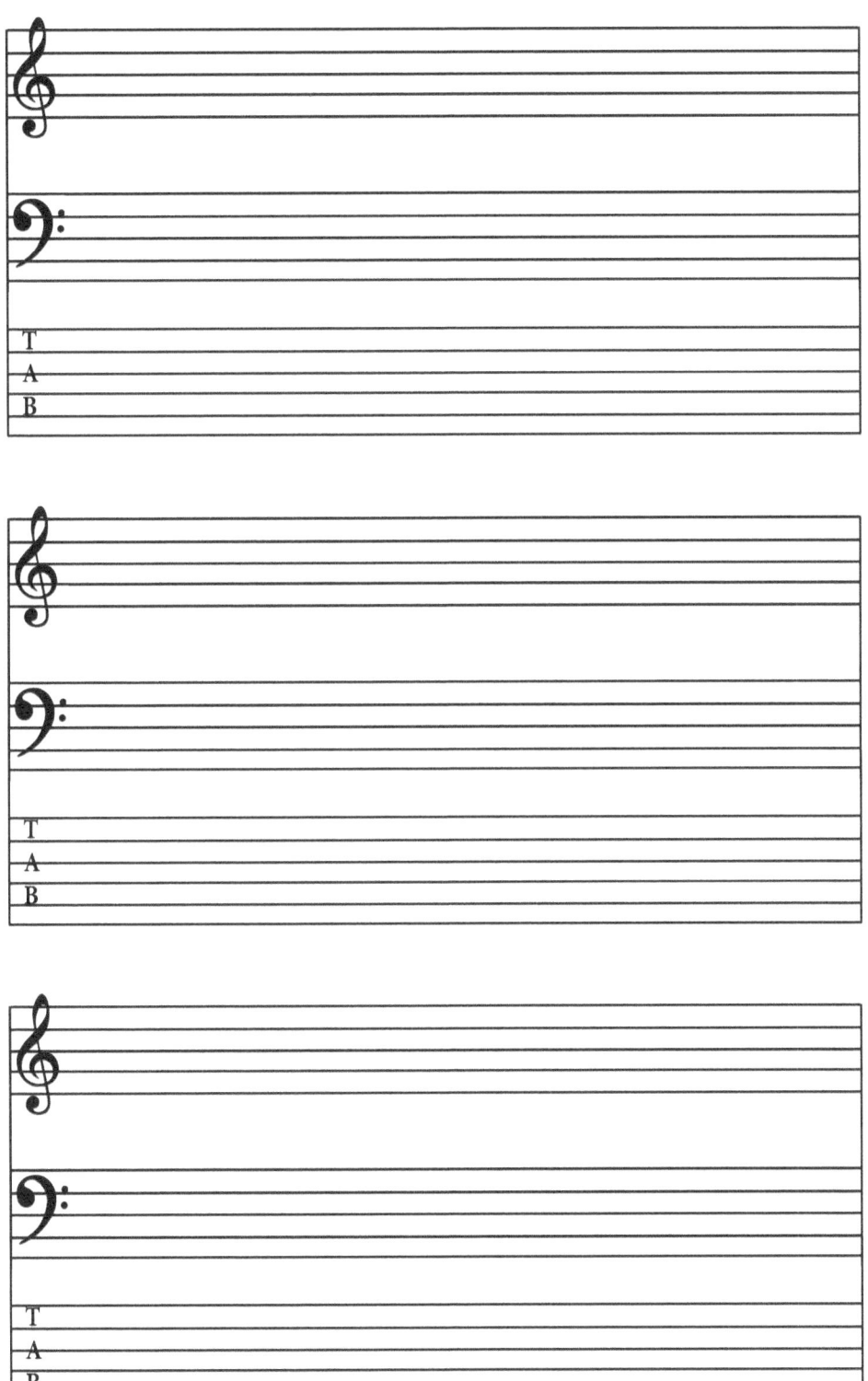

Flint must be an extremely wealthy town:
I see that each of you have bought two seats.
~Victor Borge, playing to a half-filled house in Flint, Michigan

Life is what happens while you are making other plans.
~John Lennon

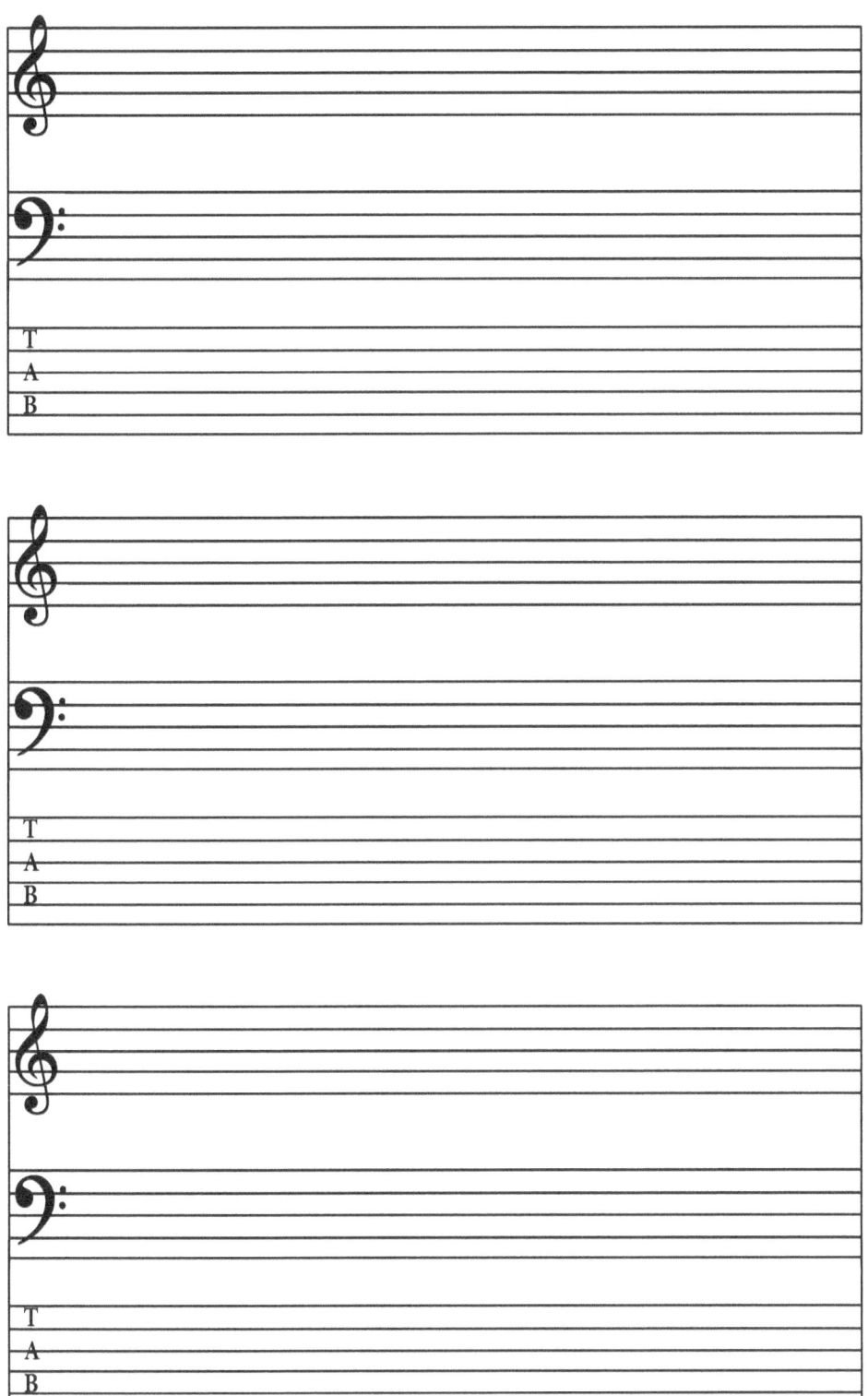

I worry that the person who thought up Muzak may be thinking up something else.
~Lily Tomlin

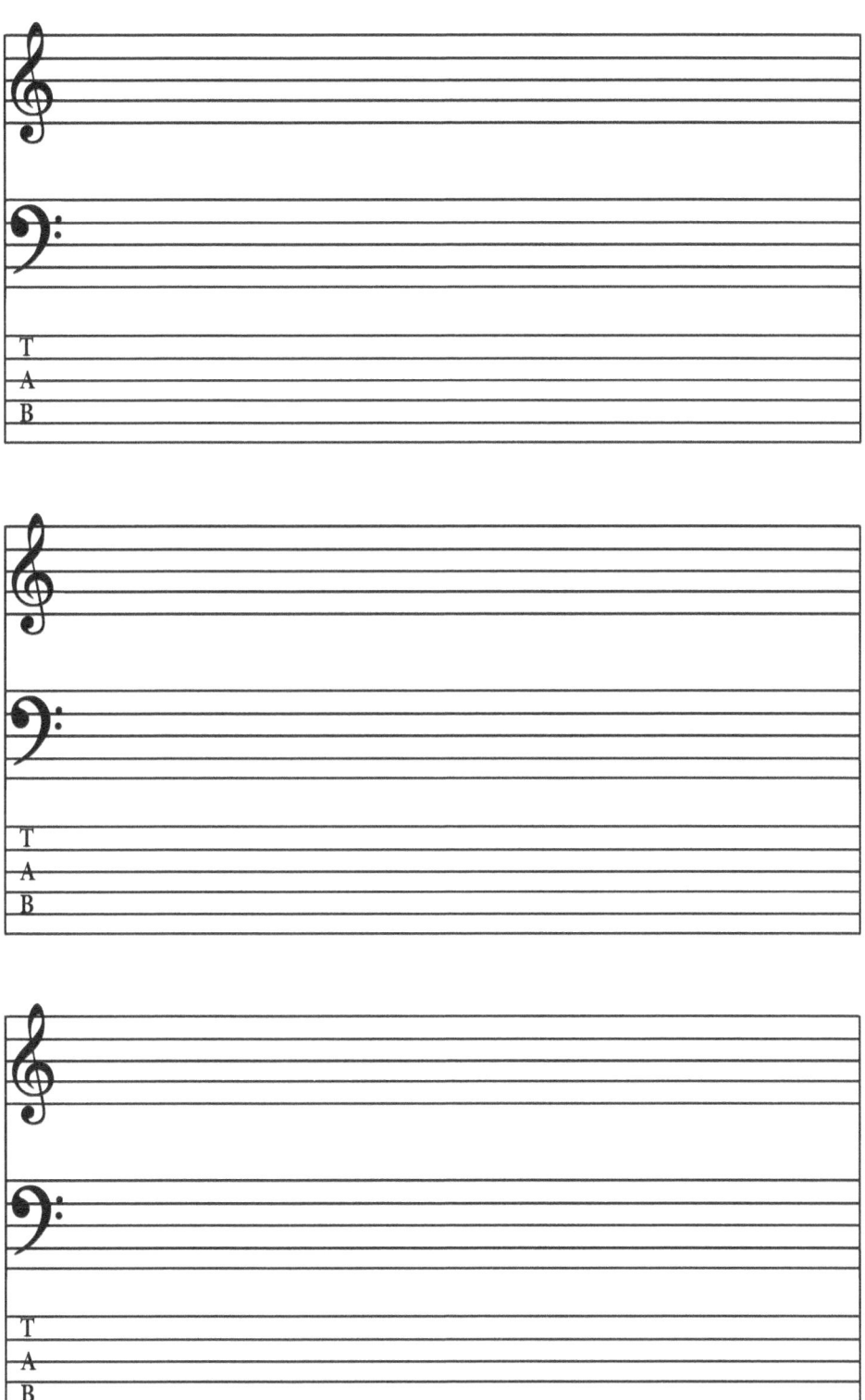

Wagner's music is better than it sounds.
~Mark Twain

It's not the writing of the lyric; it's the rewrite.
~Alan Bergman

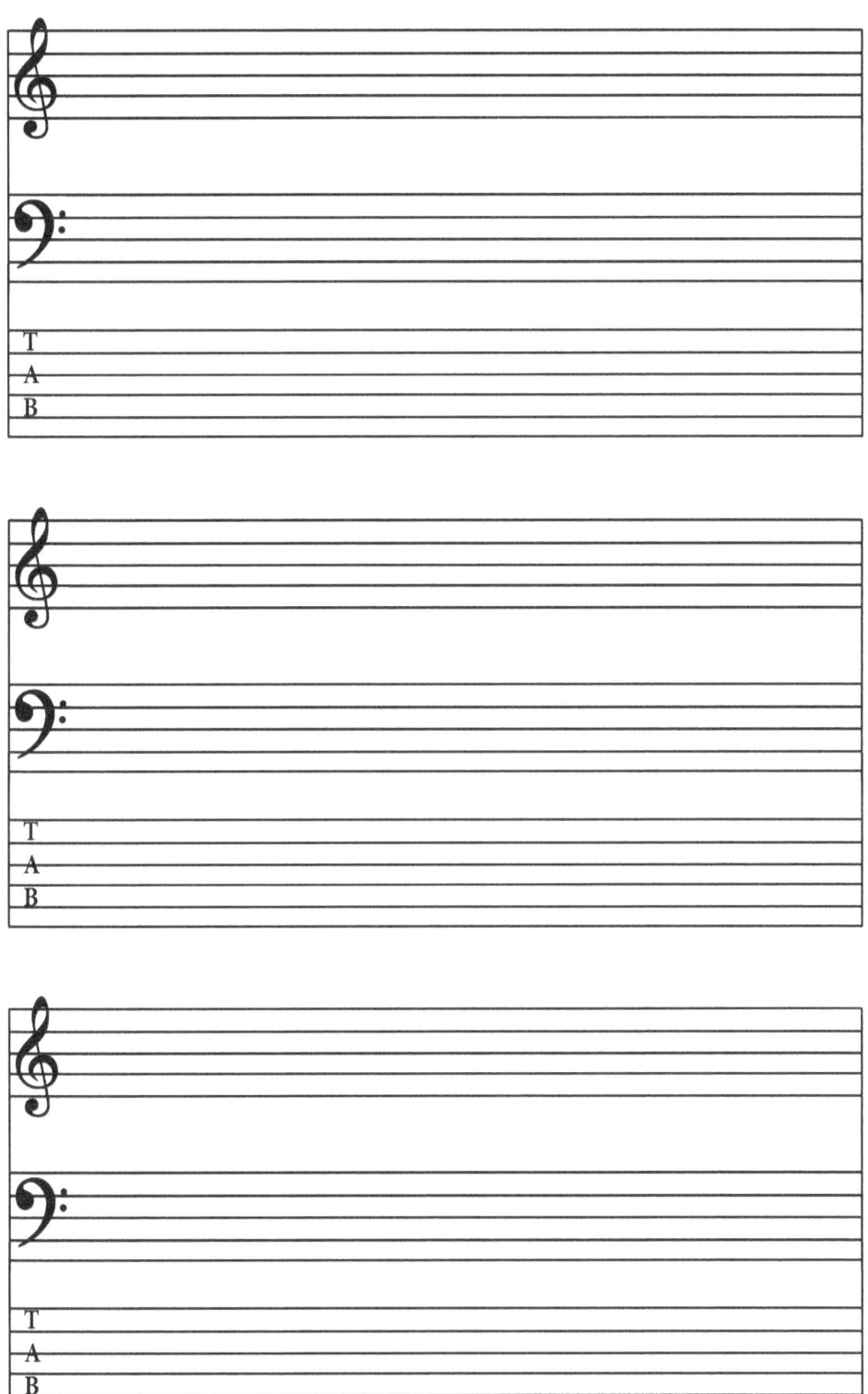

Our sweetest songs are those that tell of saddest thought.
~Percy Bysshe Shelley

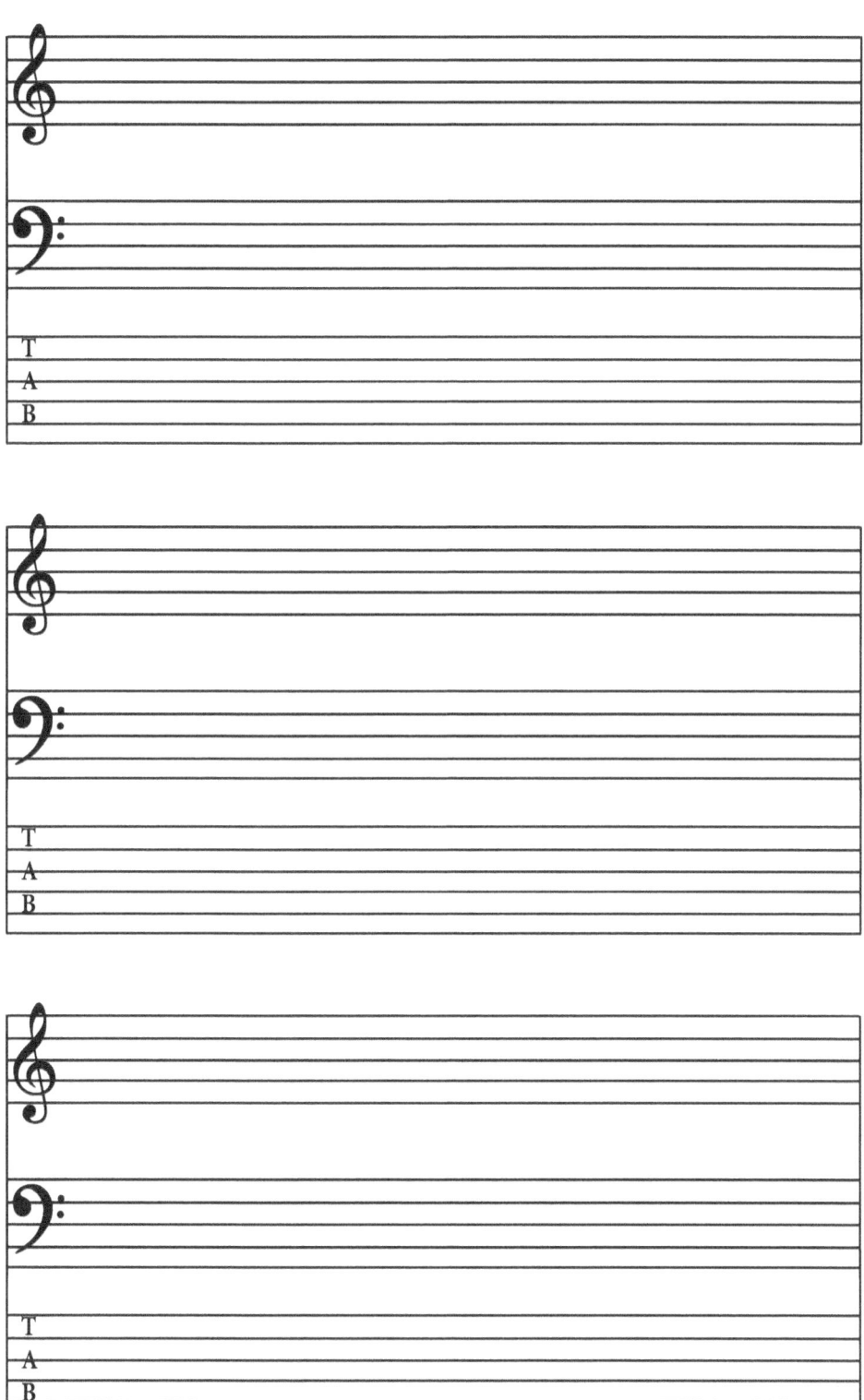

I never wanted to be famous, I only wanted to be great.
~Ray Charles

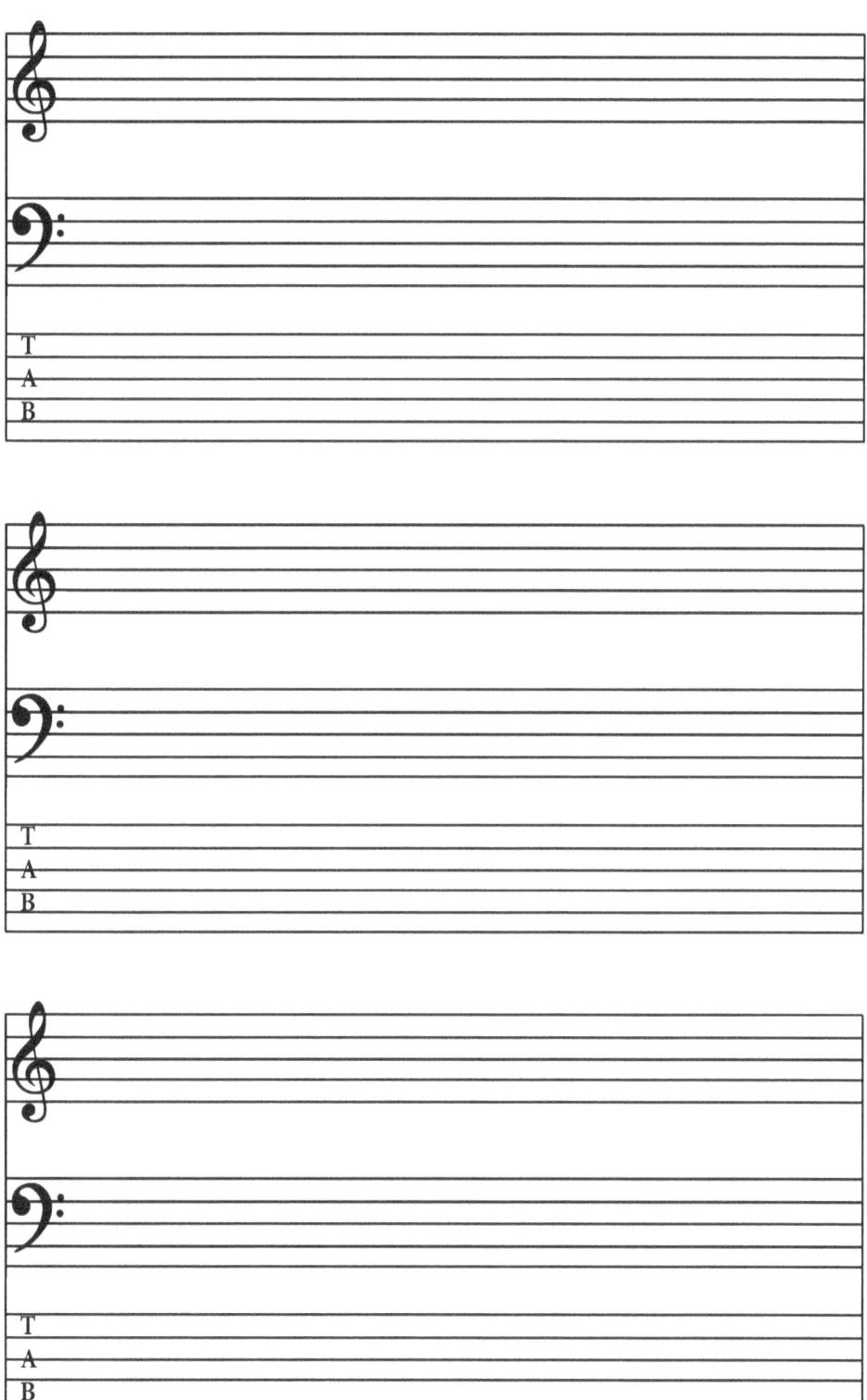

Blues is a good woman feeling bad.
~Thomas A. Dorsey

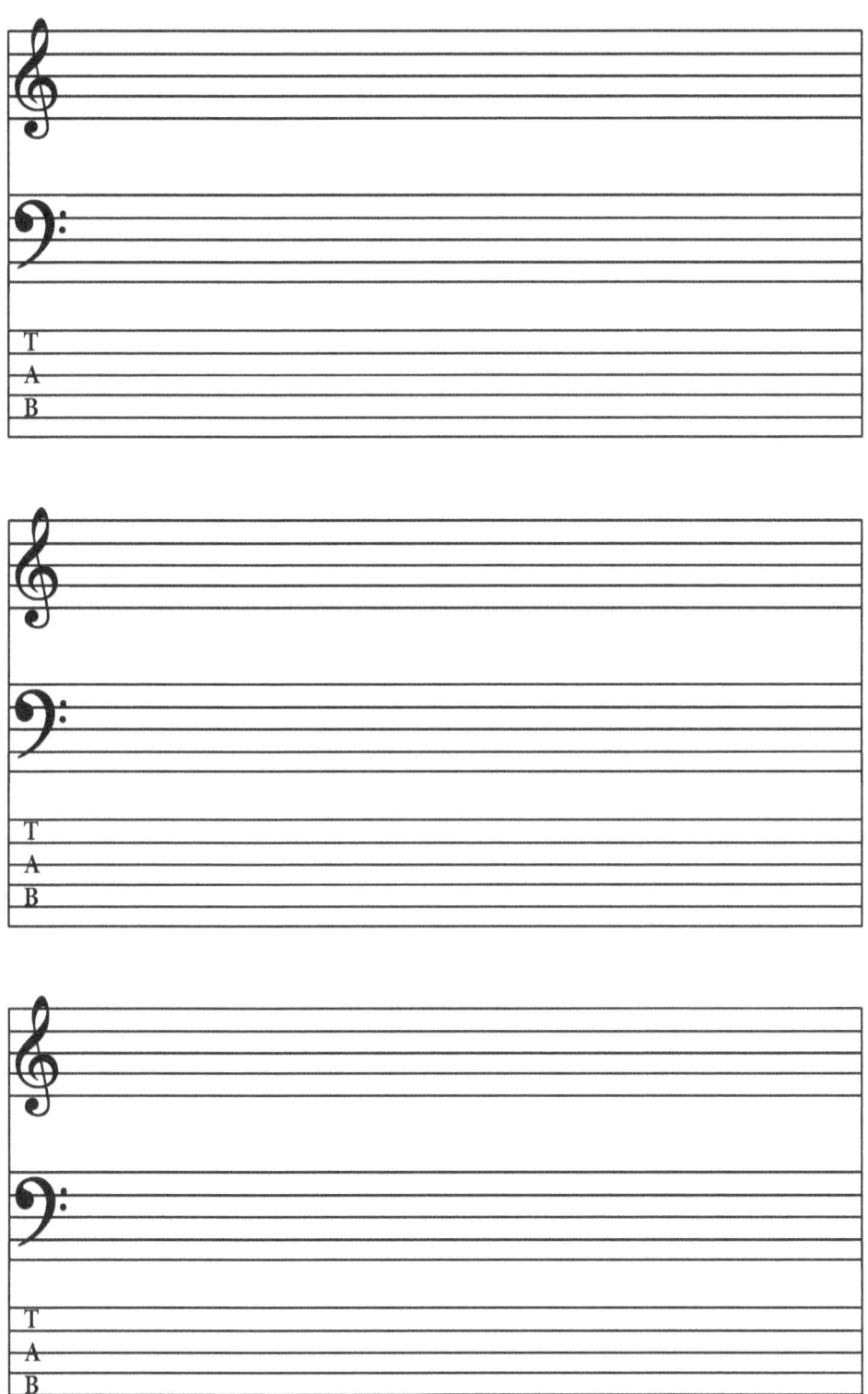

You don't get to choose how you are going to die. Or when.
You only get to choose how you are going to live. Now.
~Joan Baez

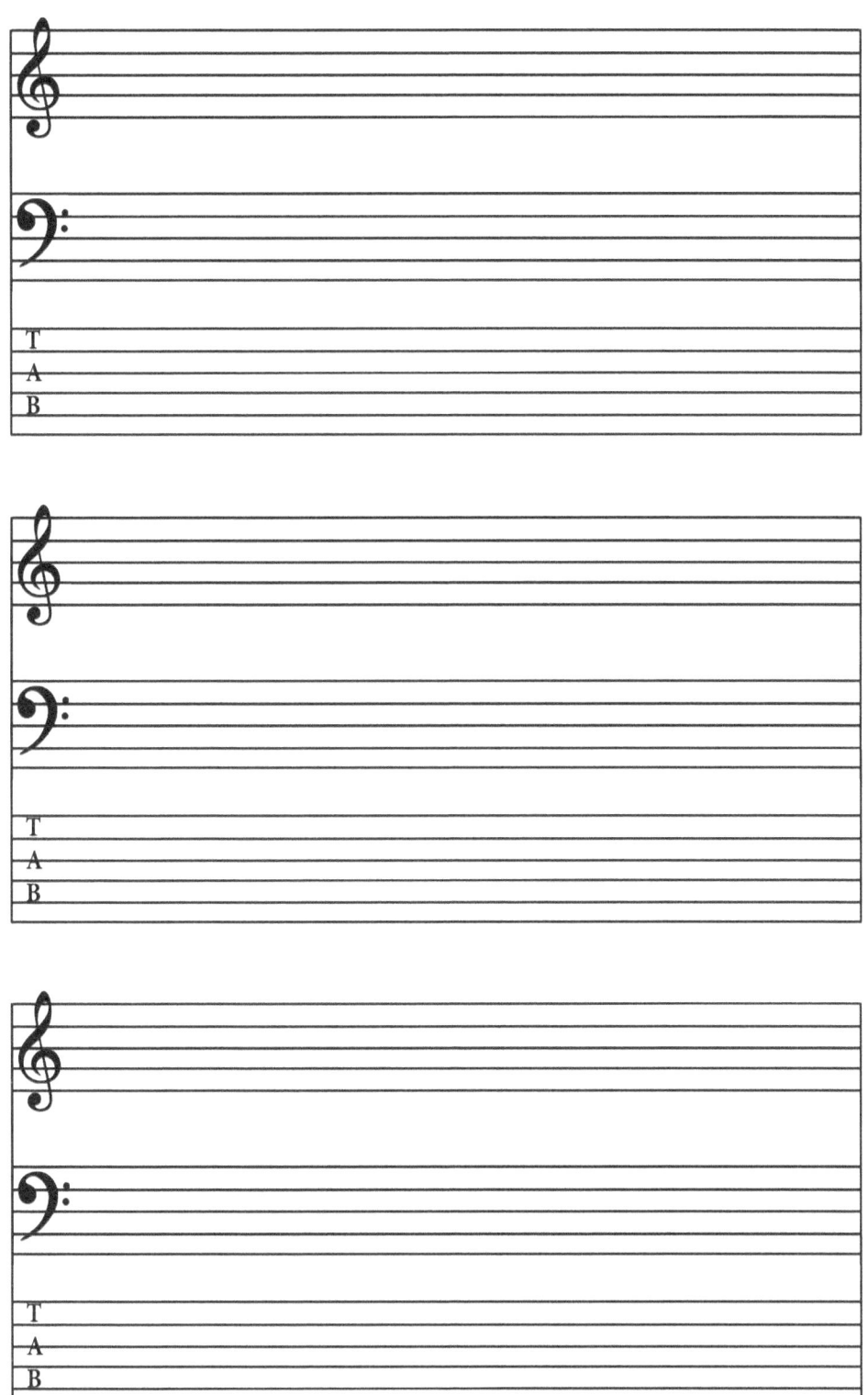

A man's screech should exceed his rasp, or what's a violin for?
~Stuart Rogers

Country music is three chords and the truth.
~Harlan Howard

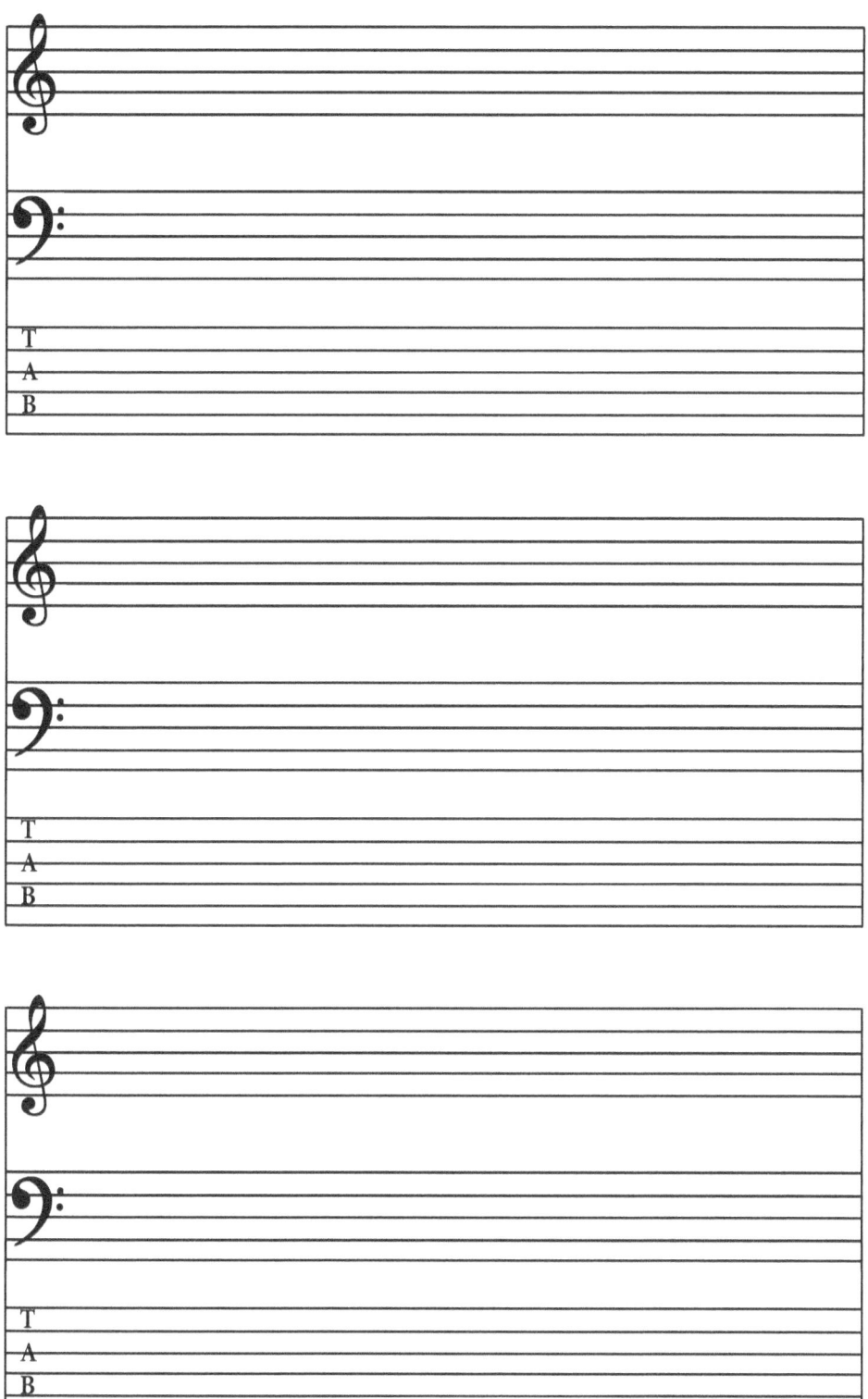

Music produces a kind of pleasure which human nature cannot do without.
~Confucius

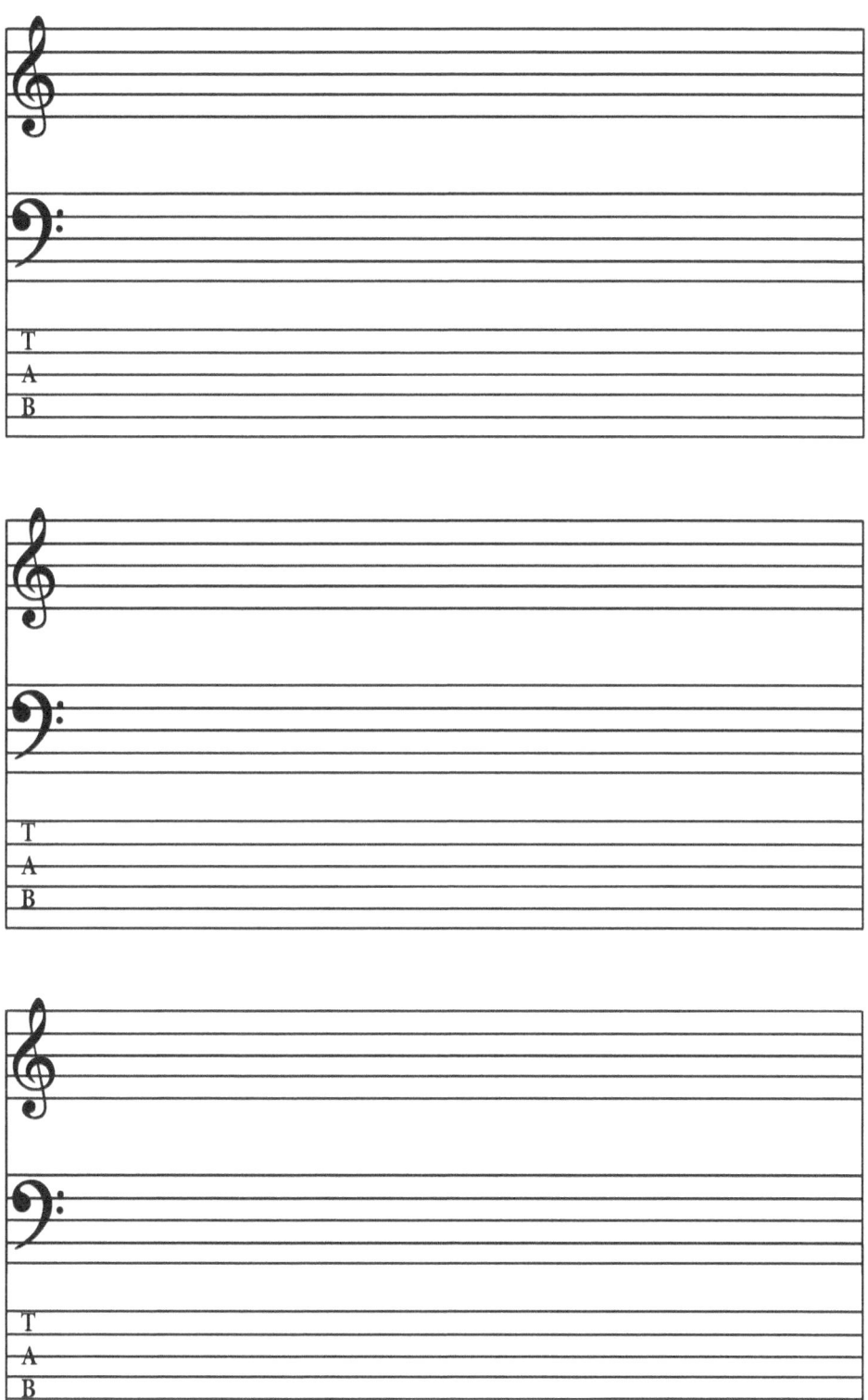

Music in the soul can be heard by the universe.
~Lao Tzu

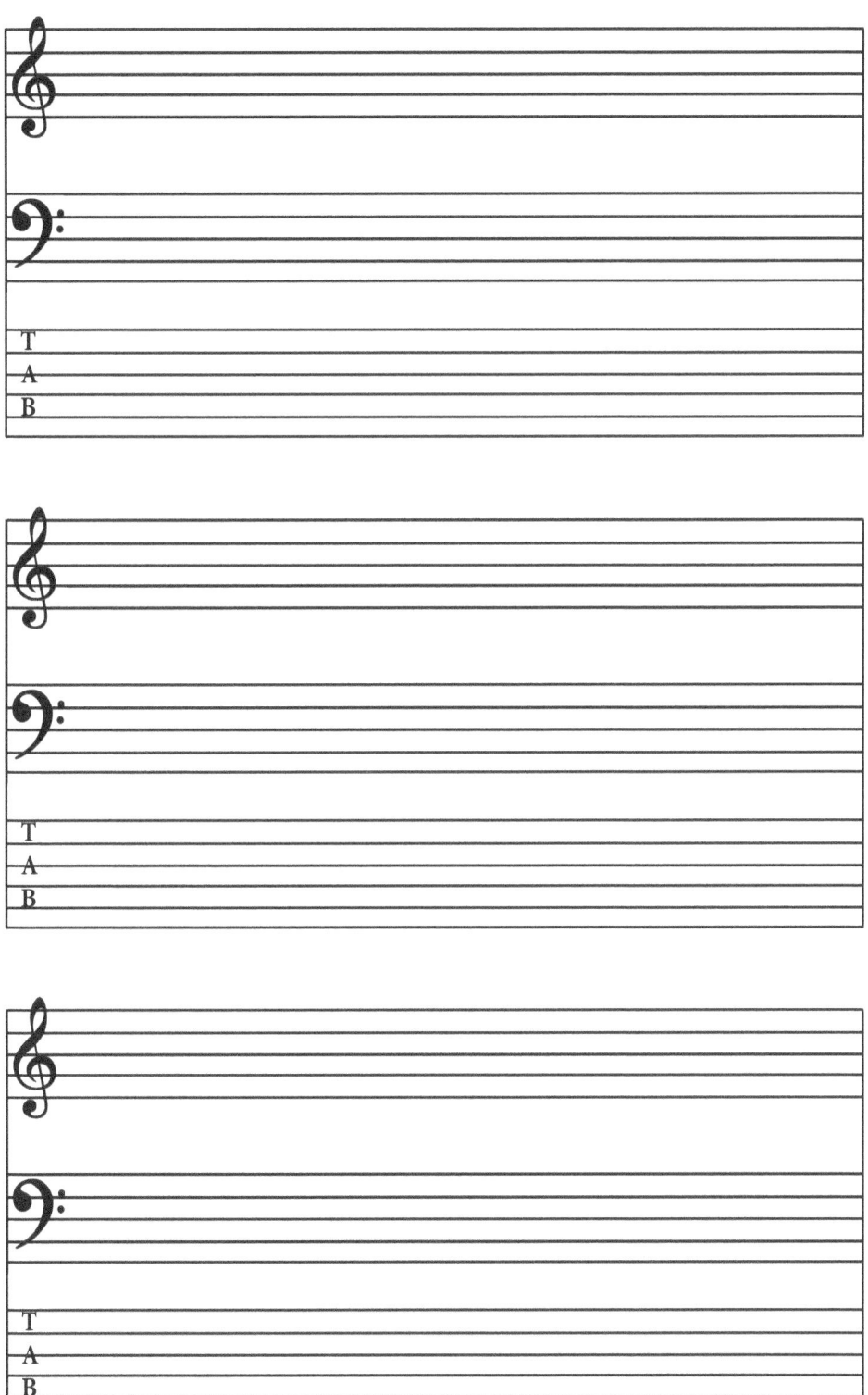

He who sings scares away his woes.
~Cervantes

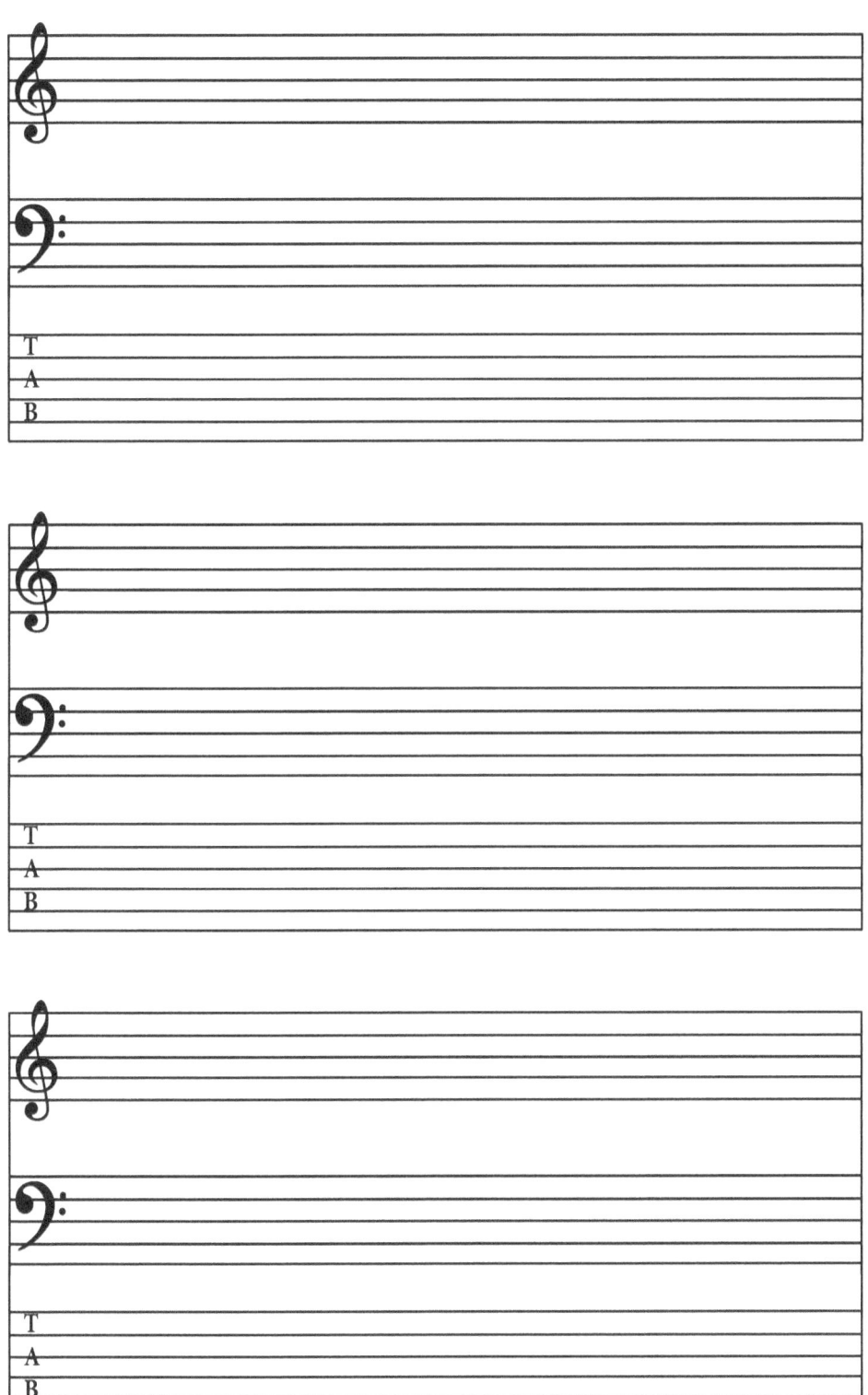

The Irish gave the bagpipes to the Scots as a joke,
but the Scots haven't got the joke yet.
~Oliver Herford

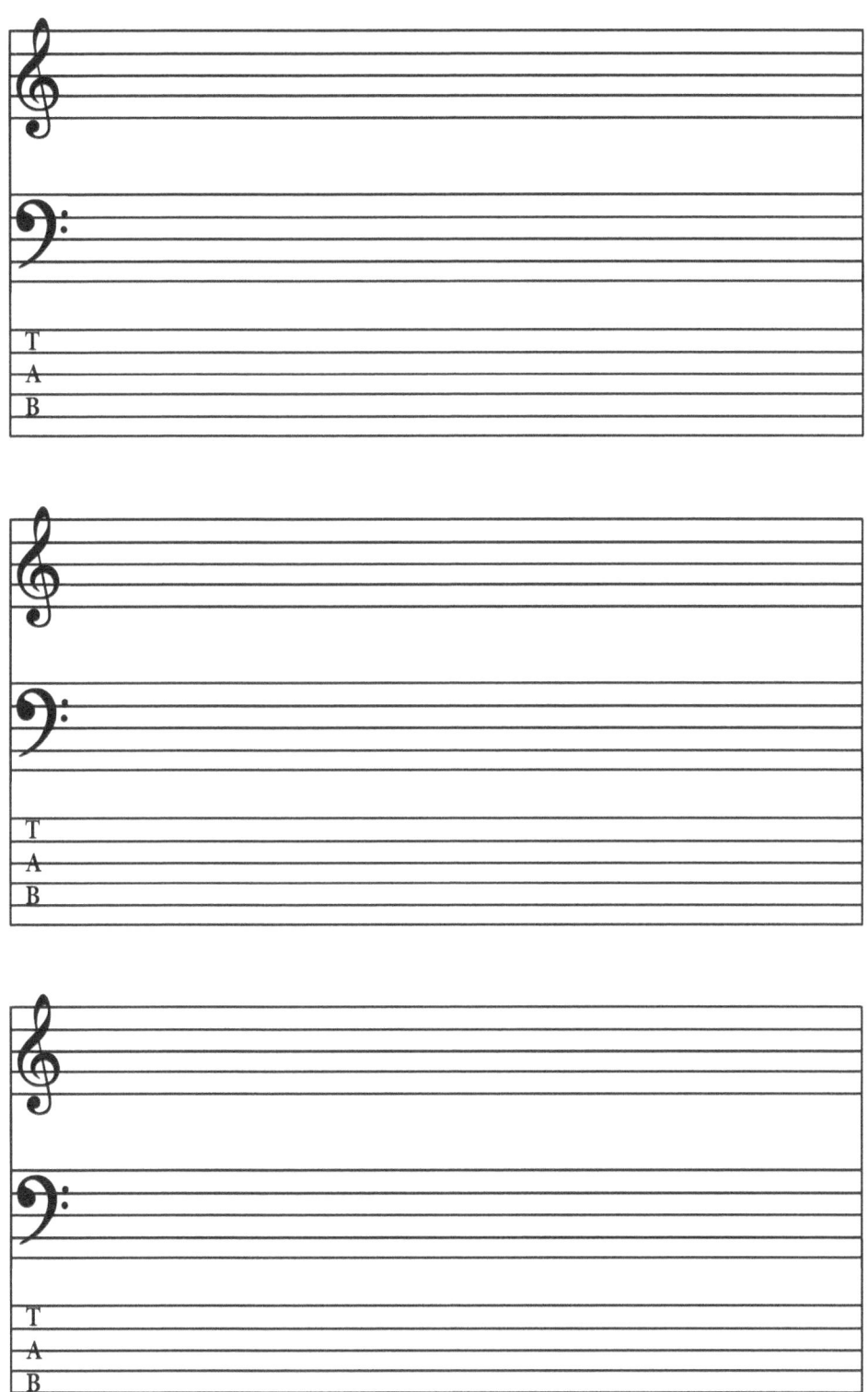

www.ingramcontent.com/pod-product-compliance
Lightning Source LLC
Chambersburg PA
CBHW030912180526
45163CB00004B/1794